THE GREAT
EPIDEMIC

Books by A. A. HOEHLING

A WHISPER OF ETERNITY

LONELY COMMAND

LAST TRAIN FROM ATLANTA

THEY SAILED INTO OBLIVION

THE FIERCE LAMBS

THE GREAT EPIDEMIC

with Mary Hoehling

THE LAST VOYAGE OF THE LUSITANIA

edited by A. A. Hoehling

THE YANKS ARE COMING

THE GREAT
EPIDEMIC

by A. A. Hoehling

With Illustrations

LITTLE, BROWN AND COMPANY

Boston   Toronto

6447

Published simultaneously in Canada
by Little, Brown & Company (Canada) Limited

PRINTED IN THE UNITED STATES OF AMERICA

*To Elizabeth Clees, and all
the "little people" whose
courage and heroism in a time
of crisis undoubtedly saved
their nation from even worse
disaster*

And God said unto Noah, The end of all flesh is come before me; for the earth is filled with violence through them; and, behold, I will destroy them with the earth . . .

Genesis, 6:13

THE GREAT
EPIDEMIC

Prologue

BY DECEMBER of that year of mingled victory and catastrophe, 1918, five hundred thousand Americans had perished in a great plague, and nearly twenty million had sickened. The world had never in history been ravaged by a killer that slew so many human beings so quickly, during but a few weeks in autumn.

This microscopic marauder that could not be seen, heard or even sensed, and was infinitely more deadly than any weapon from the crucible of the World War, was labeled almost beguilingly "Spanish influenza."

In New York State, where twenty thousand had died, Department of Health officials wrote a disheartened epitaph:

> It is questionable if any recorded epidemic has produced in a like space of time such disastrous results, yet despite the efforts of an army of research workers both here and abroad the definite causative agent of the disease remains today unknown.
>
> Until proof to the contrary is forthcoming it must be assumed that the epidemic represented a very virulent form of the same disease which has spread throughout the world from time to time for many centuries . . .

As Dr. Paul Gerhard, a sanitary engineer of New York, saw it: "An epidemic may well be likened to the sudden uprising and uproar of a gale, which in its mad fury uproots strong and healthy trees. Death comes clad in a dismal and strange raiment; it shakes the nerves of the strongest and bravest of men. People feel that the causes leading to the calamity were avoidable and that the epidemic might be due to man's indifference or carelessness in sanitary matters."

Whatever the impetus, the most skilled doctors in the world had not been able to limit the epidemic's duration by so much as one hour, or, so far as definite evidence could show, save the life of one patient who had not already been spared by the angel of death.

Their impotency in this respect was no reflection upon their abilities or their great effort, nor those of the corps of nurses and volunteers who worked — and often died — by their side. They were as powerless then to grapple with this intruder from the realm of microbes as their successors would be today. Spanish influenza, a savage strain which has never returned, would as likely destroy in the same haste and magnitude, then disappear before laboratories could first isolate the species, develop a specific vaccine, and eventually produce it in volume.

The family tree of this chameleon-like germ, however, is almost as old as the history of mankind. In 412 B.C. Hippocrates chronicled an infection resembling the flu which capped a stealthy trail of rapine by obliterating an Athenian army. These potent little germs might well have been present, if only as bacterial camp followers, during the Plague of Justinian in the sixth century A.D. The first large scourge of record, it was primarily bubonic.

Allusions became more frequent, as epidemics with some resemblance to influenza appeared every hundred or more years. In the fourteenth century the Black Death hung like a shroud over the land, eradicating several million persons, an estimated one quarter of the population of medieval Europe. The human race had never been so mightily assaulted.

The Black Death, enduring for most of the century, was, like the Plague of Justinian, characterized as bubonic. Again, however, the microscopic coyotes prowled in the wake of the main pack: cholera, typhoid, typhus, smallpox and, certainly, influenza. In the following century, the fifteenth, the flu, abandoning its often furtive, shy tactics, struck out unashamedly. Under the cloak "sweating sickness," it felled hundreds of thousands of Britons, killing sometimes within hours of its onslaught.

The Royal Navy was too sick to leave port. The Lord Mayor of London, his successor, and six aldermen all perished from this fever, which cut swathes through the habitats of the nobility but generally ignored the slums. Grief came to dwell in the stately mansions of Kensington, but the hurdy gurdy's caroling continued in Billingsgate, Limehouse and along the Whitechapel Road.

Probing among their small resources of limited tools and still more limited learning, doctors prescribed tobacco juice, lime juice, emetics, purgatives — and, in final desperation, bled their patients until they were literally pale. The impoverished, by their very inability to indulge in the luxury of medical care, recovered more surely when they did sicken. Frustrated, the followers of Aesculapius, once their bags of tricks were exhausted, could only sit by and watch the fever burn itself out.

The flu arrived in the New World from Valencia, Spain, in 1647. A new fever had disembarked to stay. And a term, bestowing dubious honor on its land of immediate origin, had been added to the medical lexicon: Spanish influenza (meaning, in Italian, simply "influence").

A celebrated research physician of London, remembered only as "Dr. Willis," in 1658 described influenza's calling cards:

. . . a feverish intemperature and whatsoever belongs to this, the heat of the praecordia, thirst, a spontaneous weariness, pain in the head, loyns and limbs, were induced from the blood growing hot and not sufficiently eventilated; hence in many, a part of the thinner blood being heated, and the rest of the liquor being only driven into confusion.

Fifty-six years after London's last and worst year of bubonic plague, 1665, Daniel Defoe added his prolific imagination to the records, and, by his descriptions of how it prostrated London and the poorer suburbs, made it seem more real than any plague up to that time. In his classic *Journal of the Plague Year* he observed:

A plague is a formidable enemy, and is armed with terrors that every man is not sufficiently fortified to resist or prepared to stand the shock against . . .
The contagion despised all medicine; death raged in every corner; and had it gone on as it did then, a few weeks more would have cleared the town of all, and everything that had a soul. Men everywhere began to despair; every heart failed them for fear; people were made desperate through the anguish of their souls, and the terrors of death sat in the very faces and countenances of the people.

For over two centuries more, all plagues — except smallpox — continued to "despise" medical efforts to subdue them. Influenza, often confused with grippe, pneumonia or other respiratory infections, has been no exception. In varying severity, it pitched its own wasting tents at Valley Forge, Shiloh, and Santiago. There was little that Army doctors could do but seek solace in Defoe's earlier rationalization, "I looked upon this dismal time to be a particular season of Divine vengeance," and wait for the Creator's ire to subside.

Noah Webster, shortly after the American Revolution, evinced scientific curiosity in influenza, which he classed as an "epidemic and pestilential disease," and reported there had been forty-four appearances since 1174. "The causes," he wrote, "most probably exist in the elements, fire, air and water for we know of no other medium by which diseases can be communicated to whole communities of people." He concluded that influenza was "evidently the effect of some insensible qualities of the atmosphere," an "electrical quality."

Influenza, like a beautiful but entirely unscrupulous woman, continued to fascinate men of medicine, especially those of the nation — Great Britain — that had been hurt so often by its deadly flirtations.

"Influenza," wrote Dr. Theophilus Thompson, of London, in 1852, "does not, like plague, desert for ages a country which it has once afflicted, nor is it accustomed, like the sweating sickness, in any marked manner to limit its attack to particular nations, or race of mankind. There is a grandeur in its constancy and immutability superior to the influence of the national habits. . . .

"The disease, moreover, exhibits in the well-ordered mansions of modern days phenomena similar to those which it presented in the time when rushes strewed the ground in the presence of our monarchs and decaying animal and vegetable matter obstructed the porticoes of the palace."

In the nineteenth century there were two pandemics of influenza, in 1847-1848 and in 1889. Both were relatively mild in America. Some medical men branded the latter wave "Chinese distemper," holding that its inception was in the dust eddying from the parched banks of the Yellow River. There was also a neighboring variety, "Russian influenza."

Some pointed an accusing finger at the volcanic ash from Mt. Krakatoa's mighty eruption of 1883. A few swore that the mysterious plague lurked in the heavens, secreted within "cosmic dust." Whatever its lair, the evil organism largely vanished again for more than a quarter of a century. Mankind, dis-

7

tracted by the mingled scientific blandishments and international Armageddon of the twentieth century, tended to forget all about influenza and many other invisible but nonetheless relentless killers.

Even when Spanish influenza had augured unmistakably that it would unleash an all-out offensive, perhaps within days, responsible officials still could not believe it. In New York City, for example, the glow of a burgeoning fever was evident when Dr. Royal S. Copeland, the city health commissioner, stated: "The city is in no danger of an epidemic."

As if in second to Dr. Copeland, the Surgeon General of the United States Navy admitted that "no indication was given of the unprecedented and frightfully fatal epidemics which were to sweep over the entire world in the autumn."

The observations of these respected authorities mirrored in part the honest incredulity of almost everyone that a plague, in 1918, could happen. The years of Justinian and even of Defoe were long gone. This was the modern age, that of man's mastery over — almost everything. These impressions, however, proved to be woven of the same gossamer as hopes four years earlier that the assassination of Archduke Franz Ferdinand would not precipitate a war or in significant measure alter the social or political future of the world and those who called it home.

When Spanish influenza finally burst its chrysalis, it created havoc and carnage for which there was no precedent. From the jungle to the polar regions, it snuffed out upwards of twenty-one million lives. Only tiny Tristan da Cunha fifteen hundred miles to the south, and far more isolated than St. Helena Island in the desolate South Atlantic, where Napoleon had languished in exile, escaped totally untouched.

No one ever quite figured out how the flu traveled such great distances and in so short a space of time. Coast Guard searching parties, for example, discovered Eskimo villages in remote, inaccessible Alaskan regions wiped out to the last adult and child.

The influenza germ was not only a Gulliver, a Marco Polo, for its peregrinating ability, but, as dubbed by some researchers, also an Arnold von Winkelried of the microbacteriological world. This analogy arose naturally enough from that Swiss hero's ability to absorb the spears of the enemy.

By October's end the Spanish influenza had "topped all records of pestilence." With insane fury, the invisible killer claimed immeasurably more lives in a matter of days than the combined armies of the world had accomplished in four years of fighting. Attrition in the United States was ten times that suffered by the American Expeditionary Force in battle. Activity in Army camp and war plant alike slowed and sometimes ceased altogether. Men and women, especially those between the ages of twenty and forty, died even as they sought medical help, which was often unobtainable. Faced with this abrupt glimmering of eternity, people became frightened, and, even as in Defoe's fiction, "sorrow and sadness sat upon every face."

Dread had seized the land as its very own. There seemed renewed evidence that the Lord, out of all patience with his brawling, fractious creatures of flesh and blood, had determined to wipe them like chaff from the face of the earth, as in the time of Noah.

In 1918 it began to appear that this microbial flood would almost accomplish the task, and with no therapeutic ark available as salvation for the pure. Had the epidemic continued its mathematical rate of acceleration, the Lord's conjectured intent might well have been consummated. Civilization could have disappeared within a few more weeks.

It was perhaps coincidence that with the advent of the Armistice of 1918, the pandemic was suddenly and providen-

9

tially stayed. The microscopic organism responsible for Spanish influenza, against which mankind possessed such little resistance, vanished. Its "visitation" had ended.

. . . And where it went no one has discovered to this day.

1

AN EPIDEMIC has to start *somewhere*. And one accusing medical finger was focused in 1918 upon an otherwise improbable dot in the prairie: Fort Riley, Kansas.

This old outpost had mushroomed since the declaration of war into a military babel, sprawling over twenty thousand acres, classroom for a hodgepodge of people, horses, machines and — things. Within its teeming precincts it had even spawned another reservation: Camp Funston.

While the scope and the appearance of Fort Riley would have been shockingly unfamiliar to a General Custer, the weather hadn't changed a bit since his cavalry thundered across the badlands. The troops froze under winter blizzards and parboiled beneath a summer sun which sometimes sent the mercury as high as 107°.

As soon as the ice in the Kansas River thawed and snow-drifts were absorbed into the hard soil, blinding dust storms commenced. And this Saturday, March 9, it was apparent that another such storm was churning towards Fort Riley. By noon, the sky was ominously black. Sagebrush atop the bluffs along the post's northern boundary bent under a skirling, rising wind.

Cavalrymen and infantrymen, artillerymen and engineers, signalmen, hospital corpsmen, bakers, butchers, ordnance men, veterinarians and company clerks all beat a retreat to their barracks — drafty and insecure refuge against dust, cold or anything else though these barracks were.

Now, there was nothing to do but wait out the fury of a Western plains dust storm. Trucks came to a stop on the Golden Belt Highway, which ribboned past the encampment. Trains on the paralleling Union Pacific tracks threw on their air brakes and rasped to a banging halt. Headlights could not penetrate the storm. The rickety trolleycars linking the military post with neighboring Manhattan and Junction City, which even in crystal-clear weather hardly proceeded at a dangerous clip, slowed to a snail's pace.

The thousands of horses and mules attached to the cavalry, remount and maintenance units sneezed in their stalls and tugged at their halters. The vast quantity of these quadrupeds at Fort Riley had, as a matter of fact, created an almost insoluble hygienic problem: nine thousand tons of manure a month. In desperation, the mule skinners could do nothing but burn the mountainous, odorous heaps. A noxious smoke haze over the post was the inevitable result of this daily disposal. Sifting ashes contributed to an almost continual drum roll of respiratory coughings and wheezings — and also a monotony of crude if obvious humor.

For three hours the storm howled at gale force. Then it passed, leaving everywhere a cerement of dust and dirt — and the ashes from the burning manure piles.

Now, the sun was shining again. The amorphous monster that was a military organization stirred and was roused to full life. Captains called to lieutenants, and lieutenants relayed the command down to their sergeants, who bellowed from barracks to barracks: "Clean up!"

Bucket and broom brigades were soon attacking the unsightly cover deposited by the wind. Their labors continued past midnight, and into the dark, quieter hours of predawn Sunday.

By afternoon, one would not have guessed that the post had been lashed and fouled by the storm. The sergeants rasped their leathery "Count off!" as the men lined up to drill. Others took their places on the firing range. The endless truck convoys pounded once more over the Golden Belt Highway and the whistle of train locomotives again sounded their reassuring matins and, later, vespers.

Of all the officers of ascending rank at Fort Riley who might be affected by the vicissitudes of weather or changes in the daily routine, perhaps Colonel Edward R. Schreiner, forty-five-year-old surgeon, was the most directly concerned — and perturbed. He had never been too pleased with the health situation or future prospects at this makeshift, wasteland home of twenty-six thousand hapless souls.

He was in full, applauding agreement with Surgeon General William C. Gorgas, who had testified only two months earlier before the Senate Military Affairs Committee that overcrowding was rampant in all military camps. The white-haired veteran of the battle against yellow fever had repeated what he had already cautioned: that mobilization should have been delayed "two or three months" for better facilities.

With lack of heat, hot water and even latrines, Dr. Schreiner was gratified that the health of his command was as good as it was. There had been spotty eruptions of pneumonia, measles, grippe, mumps, and even two hundred cases of spinal meningitis. To soldiers such as Private John Lewis Barklay, of Holden, Missouri, in training at this "dismal place," it appeared that "it got so that as soon as they hauled down one quarantine flag they ran up another one in its place." And the hospital's chief nurse, pretty Lieutenant Elizabeth Harding, sighed, "I have spent the coldest winter of my life."

The cold and the scattering of infectious diseases did not seem to Dr. Schreiner too dear a price to pay for the primitive surroundings. After all, the 3068-bed capacity of his hospital — a complex of old limestone buildings, brick structures and clapboard barracks — had never been approached.

On Monday morning, March 11, before breakfast time, the duty sergeant at Hospital Building 91, once host to the sickened backwash of the Spanish-American War, had a caller. Albert Gitchell, a company cook, complained of a "bad cold." He was feverish, suffered from a sore throat, headache and muscular pains. Gitchell was quickly banished to a contagious ward. Hardly had a corpsman put a thermometer in the soldier's mouth when Corporal Lee W. Drake from the First Battalion, Headquarters Transportation Detachment, reported to the same admitting desk in Building 91. His symptoms, even to a 103° fever, were identical with Gitchell's.

Two cases with a rubber stamp similarity could have been coincidence. However, when Sergeant Adolph Hurby came coughing in moments later, the duty corpsman called for the chief nurse. By the time Lieutenant Harding had arrived at Building 91 two other sick soldiers were awaiting admission. Miss Harding knew she was confronted with a potentially grave situation. She cranked the wall phone.

"Colonel," she commenced with concern.

Surgeon Schreiner, a sober, meticulous officer, did not wait to shave, comb his mustache, or even snap the hooks and eyes of his uniform's choker collar. He hurried out of his quarters and shook the nodding driver of his motorcycle and sidecar, which was always standing by. Soon he was examining his first patient, shortly, his second, his third, and so on. By breakfast time, the telltale medical manifestations were as obvious to

Colonel Schreiner as the inscriptions in a family Bible. With the aid of his assistants, he was noting on chart after chart, except for minor variations:

Fever 104°. Low pulse, drowsiness and photophobia. Conjunctivae reddened and mucous membranes of nose, throat and bronchi, evidence of inflammation.

There was little doubt in Dr. Schreiner's mind that the Army post had been hit with influenza. By noon, 107 patients had been admitted to the hospital.

Cultures and later observations further confirmed Dr. Schreiner's initial diagnosis. There was present, for example, the bacillus which Dr. Richard Pfeiffer, a Berlin professor and pathologist, had isolated in 1892. He believed this hemophilic, or blood-nourished, bacteria to be the cause of influenza, although other bacteriologists disputed his conclusion.

In the cultures made at Camp Funston pneumococci and streptococci were also observed. Like Pfeiffer's bacillus, they inspired the question anew: Did one or more of these microscopic species spark the infection or were they merely bacterial hangers-on?

Other symptoms, not associated with the more general respiratory ailments, developed: "cervical and general lymphadenitis and nystagmus," or glandular disturbances complicated by aberrations of the patient's eyes. There was an evident depression in mononuclear cells. In fact, Dr. Schreiner was struck by the profound depression, a slowing down in all bodily functions and reactions, including the heart action. This in itself was a seeming paradox, under the stimulus of fever.

But what was the cause of this "explosive outbreak"?

Dr. Schreiner reflected on Saturday's dust storm, the burning manure, the air laden with a Pandora's box of poisonous irritants. He knew his medical history sufficiently to associate

15

dust with many ailments, especially those of a respiratory nature. Until the past spring he had served on the Mexican border and was well aware of the medical problems spurred by dirt, dust and dry heat. It was worse at Fort Riley, however, because not only were those enemies to health present but the complication was added of excessive crowding in substandard dwellings.

. . . By the end of the week, 522 cases had been recorded at Camp Funston. Advisories from Dr. Gorgas's office showed that Camp Kearny, California, Camp Johnston, Florida, Camp Lee, Virginia, Camp McClellan, Alabama, Camp Sevier, South Carolina, and Fort Oglethorpe, Georgia, had also experienced some flu during the past few weeks. The Navy reported three hundred flu-pneumonia cases on ships berthed at East Coast ports. Even the stone walls of penitentiaries did not make a bulwark against the bacteria. Five hundred of the nineteen hundred inmates of San Quentin sickened in April and May, three of them dying. Within five weeks the "explosive outbreak" at Camp Funston had spent itself, after 1127 soldiers had been stricken. The forty-six fatalities were attributed to pneumonia.

By no stretch of the imagination, except on the part of those morbidly apprehensive, could the March infection at Army camps be interpreted as the forerunner of a plague. Nonetheless Dr. Schreiner wrested concessions from the War Department: screens for kitchen windows, oil for the dusty roadways, and better plumbing. The torch, however, continued to be applied to the mountains of manure. The smoke pall, with its acrid burden of ashes, mantled the entire military reservation with the persistence of a bad memory.

Training continued. In May the 89th and 92d Divisions emerged from their trial by ice, fire, and fever as military entities. They sailed for France, where they would augment the strength of the American Expeditionary Force to nearly five hundred thousand.

The doughboys, however, brought more with them than their packs and rifles. At Brest and St.-Nazaire, where members of the 92d disembarked, influenza made an appearance in May. It crossed France in far faster time than was associated with the speed of the beleagured country's railroads to attack A.E.F. headquarters at Chaumont. There, 132 cases were recorded in twelve days.

This outbreak in France, whether or not another United States import, was difficult to label. Surgeons, busy with the flotsam of battle, had scant time for borderline determinations between flu, pneumonia, grippe, or, indeed, colds.

French troops suffered with *la grippe* in late April and May at Villers-sur-Coudun, at Tours, at Toulon, and also at Brest. At the latter port there was a little doubt that the *poilus* had contracted the annoying aches, chills and coughs from their American allies as they disembarked.

The British also received a part of these woes. Tommies packed the germs in their old kit bags and toted them across the English Channel. Soon gentlemen like Harry Furniss of the Garrick Club were writing to *The Times* of London, suggesting remedies for the "Flanders grippe":

> The specific is simple. It is to take snuff which arrests and slays the insidious bacillus with great effect . . . and during the last few days I have had my own capacious snuffbox replenished.

The Royal Navy counted 10,313 flu cases. King George V himself came down with the sniffles this miserable spring, as Britons were plagued as well by bombing raids, food shortages and daily casualty lists that allowed no one to forget the Great War. Scotland was infected with a tougher breed of Flanders grippe. At the end of May, pneumonia-flu deaths had tripled from a few weeks previously to 107 a week.

The June probings of influenza, like those of a pugilist who has not summoned his confidence and who as yet is not sure of his power, nonetheless made some medical men stop what they were doing — and think.

"In the midst of perfect health," wrote Dr. Herbert French in a report to the British Ministry of Health, "in a circumscribed community, such as a barracks or a school, the first case of influenza would occur, and then within the next few hours or days a large proportion — and occasionally every single individual of that community — would be stricken down with the same type of febrile illness, the rate of spread from one to another being remarkable. The patient would be seized rapidly, or almost suddenly, with a sense of such prostration as to be utterly unable to carry on with what he might be doing; from sheer lassitude he would be obliged to lie down where he was, or crawl with difficulty back to bed so that barrack rooms which the day before had been full of bustle and life, would now be converted wholesale into one great sick room, the number of sick developing so rapidly that hospitals were within a day or two so overfull that fresh admissions were impossible."

While temperatures might soar to 104°, patients nonetheless slept well, wishing only to be left alone. With aspirin, quinine and salicylates, they were up and about their business in a few days. By late June, the flu had dug in as if to stay beside the weary trench soldiers. Exposure, filth, overcrowding and all the bedfellows of death had hung out the welcome sign for the new virus — if virus it was — the length of the western front.

The crippling and often lethal mustard gas itself, with known chemical properties of mutation, was believed to have played a role in altering and toughening the existing influenza strain. The French declared the malady, whatever the effect of the war and its weapons upon it, to be "purulent bronchitis." It was "sandfly fever," said the Italians. *"Blitz Katarrh"* was the object of the Germans' guttural invective.

Throughout the Kaiser's unhappy nation there stalked the dual *Götterdämmerung* of epidemic and hunger. In Berlin, 160,000 residents were ill with flu. Almost all streetcar motormen were sick, while Emperor Wilhelm himself, even as his English cousin King George, had fallen prey. Epidemics were reported in Strasbourg, Munich, Jena, Bonn and Cologne. Soon this illness had crossed the borders into Austria-Hungary and then Switzerland. The tiny Swiss army was put to bed almost to the last private.

Europe was like one vast laboratory test tube, and the very depletion of those who lived and fought there left a broth in which any fungus or pestilence could grow with almost the speed of light.

When such a broth foamed up to the point where it must burst its retort, it would inevitably spill over and spread out in all directions. The Atlantic Ocean, which apparently had been the initial invasion route, was no bulwark. As a matter of fact, the pestilence effected clear sailing across the Pacific Ocean — coming ashore at the Hawaiian Islands, among other ports. By June 26, there were 370 cases at Schofield Barracks, Honolulu, and eleven deaths.

Influenza was not confined to the tedious caravan routes of old. It could go aboard destroyers, or hop into fighter planes. Overland there were fast trains such as the Orient Express, the Flying Scotsman, or the Twentieth Century Limited.

If the micro-organism was not content with these deluxe conveyances, it appeared to possess as well its own mysterious mode of communication and lightning infection. No hypodermic needle yet devised was so sure in its capacity to inoculate.

2

BY JULY, Spanish influenza was a seasoned traveler and an increasingly bold one. Leaping about Asia with desultory abandon, it rolled over much of China "like a tidal wave," according to Dr. Arthur Stanley, of the Shanghai Health Department. It also jumped to Japan, where it was tagged "wrestler's fever," and among other depredations nullified the effectiveness of the Imperial Navy.

The Oriental eruption set medical men to debating its origin. Had Asia spawned its own brand, or had the flu been introduced from Europe or the United States? Because of its prevalence in China some pathologists rushed to the conclusion that coolies imported to France to dig trenches had brought the bacteria with them. So some called the epidemic "Chungking fever."

Spain was infected. The hottest fever spots were Madrid, Badajoz and Seville. Off Spain's southern coast, upon Britain's rocky bastion Gibraltar, funeral processions winding day and night attested to the seriousness of the infestation. The "Rock's" apes also were perishing, seemingly in sober fulfillment of the long-ago prophecy that when the apes died, Gibraltar would pass from British possession.

Christiania, Norway, reported more than two thousand cases. Puerto Rico was also suffering from an attack, as were Sierra Leona, Reykjavik, Athens, and Nome, Alaska. There was no geographical pattern or, necessarily, a clear-cut path of transmission.

In London, the week of July 8, there were 287 reported influenza deaths, twenty-eight times the number of three weeks previously. Birmingham counted 126 fatalities. The "sweating sickness" of five centuries earlier was vividly brought to mind.

And this sickness had already taken a serious turn from June, when the fever was more like distant, fitful lightning on a summer night. For example, doctors found in the lungs a pathological nightmare: not only acute congestion, but diffuse hemorrhaging, miliary abscesses, croupous pneumonia, passive edema, sometimes purulent bronchiolitis and even complete lung collapse.

Dr. Herbert French of London, who had reported in June, was awed to note that "the lungs were invariably heavier than normal and often greatly so, the increased weight being a feature of the lower lobes rather than the upper . . . the lung lesions, complex or variable, struck one as being quite different in character to anything one had met with at all commonly in the thousands of autopsies one has performed during the last 20 years. Broncho-pneumonia was very frequently a part of the picture complex but it was not like the common broncho-pneumonia of ordinary years."

India, where the flu already was described as "severe," had exported her own strain of infection. On July 16, nearly two dozen ill Indians were removed from a ship at Brest. They were quarantined at the United States Navy's Base Hospital No. 2. Within a few days, the fever had spread to fifty-five enlisted men at the Navy's establishment and to nineteen nurses, apparently a fresh wave of the May disturbance in the same port. General Pershing, however, denied there was any infection among the A.E.F. Elsie Janis, the petite entertainer, abed in Paris with some type of lung congestion, wasn't so sure about the Commander-in-Chief's opinion.

These thrusts of the microscopic world, nonetheless, were overshadowed by the heady news that Germany was reeling in defeat. Ludendorff's summer offensive blunted, his troops were moving ponderously back towards the Rhine.

In America, "Everybody Sing" campaigns and "Liberty Sings" whooped up bond rallies and promoted living at a giddy and continuing unreal pace. Unnoticed amidst the harmony and general excitement were hints that a "visitation" of microbes might not be many days distant. Health authorities, for example, had been fumigating incoming ships at Boston, New York and other East Coast ports. The country of origin had been Spain alone — until August 12.

That warm Monday, the Norwegian liner *Bergensfjord* poked in through the mists of the Lower Bay and shortly docked at the bustling, sprawling Army Base in Brooklyn. It had been a dreadful voyage. At least a hundred passengers had been stricken with an illness "resembling influenza." Four had died and been buried at sea, hastily, with as little ceremony as possible. The day and night efforts of the crew to swab the decks, douse the corridors and even spray the air with a choking brew of creosote and ammonia had not stanched the epidemic, but only increased the discomfiture and apprehension of the frightened passengers.

Eleven semiconscious travelers were taken on stretchers from the ship and transferred to ambulances. The latter, bells clanging, hastened to the Norwegian Hospital, also in Brooklyn. There, within a few hours, Mrs. Jensine Olsen, one of the eleven, died. She had been on her way to Flint, Michigan, to meet her husband.

22

August continued, amidst continued exultation in the United States — the A.E.F. was "winning the war," and who, indeed, had ever doubted they would, from the Yanks' very first disembarkation in France?

In Boston the summer had been hot, dusty — excessively dry was the verdict of the United States Weather Bureau, which had measured but 8.13 inches of rain in four months. The city was crowded with soldiers, sailors and those who had swarmed into the area's beehive complex of shipyards. Few were more conscious of this crammed condition than Dr. William M. Bryan, Public Health Service sanitation officer for the First Naval District. Within and without the Navy's installations were people, hordes of people — so many in these, it seemed to Dr. Bryan, that every other structure of Boston was blotted into an indistinct background.

To house the Navy's own human sea were the most dishearteningly rattletrap facilities — obsolete, Dr. Bryan was certain, in McKinley's administration. Cracked toilets, lack of drinking fountains and even soap, lack of rattraps for a rodent pack which seemed sometimes as menacing as the German army — these were but some of the obvious deficiencies at the Navy Yard. In July there had been 964 accidents — some minor but the majority serious, and, in Bryan's estimation, "inexcusable."

The prime pesthole was the euphemism listed as "Receiving Ship." Not a vessel at all, it was a naval barracks and eating area in South Boston, within the drafty, odorous confines of Commonwealth Pier. Lately its overflow had spilled across Summer Street to the lofts of the Army Stores Building.

Men awaiting assignment, men just detached from their ships, and others on duty at the First Naval District — all were "guests" of the Receiving Ship, some nights as many as seven thousand enlisted personnel. Captain William A. Edgar, medical officer of the landlocked "ship," like Dr. Bryan, could only hold his breath and hope. Here, they knew, was an unusually fertile breeding ground for a harvest of trouble.

Influenza had been probing here and there, on land and sea. Presently it was reported on United States Navy vessels at Queenstown, Gibraltar, Plymouth, England, and at Pearl Harbor, in addition to several French ports. Even on the lonely station at Vladivostok, the fever sought out and then assaulted the U.S.S. *Brooklyn.* The flu, Dr. Bryan advised Captain Edgar, could sail into Boston Harbor unchallenged, at any time, with no warning.

Life and its conveniences were far more felicitous at the Chelsea Naval Hospital. Its modern red-brick structures overlooked Boston Harbor from high breezy ground and had a capacity for 1236 patients. There were little problems, nonetheless. On August 30, Captain Norman J. Blackwood, the commanding officer, dictated a letter to the chief supply clerk at the Bureau of Medicine and Surgery. He desired to replace his official Ford car with a vehicle more befitting the dignity of his position. Previous requests had gone unanswered.

Dr. Bryan this day was also writing to Washington.

> Influenza [he commenced] is markedly increasing as is shown by the fact that for the week ending August 15 there was one case, the week ending August 22, there were eight cases, and for the week ending August 29, there were 52 cases, of which 38 occurred in the last 24 hours.
>
> The congestion of the ship as well as the repeated intercourse with the civilian population is believed to be a menace to the health of the personnel and may have its influence upon the present prevalence of influenza.

Before sending off his report, Dr. Bryan was compelled to amend his totals. Last-minute figures revealed that fifty-eight, not thirty-eight, cases had occurred in the past twenty-four hours.

24

One by one, the ambulances soon snorted up the cinder path to Chelsea Naval Hospital carrying the fevered men from the Receiving Ship. Captain Blackwood knew influenza when he saw it. And now he was seeing it — in possibly pandemic proportions. The patients manifested symptoms as definite as a textbook: chills and fever, sharp pains in the back and legs; often a flaming red throat; sometimes paroxysms of coughing; labored breathing; profuse sweating. Prostration was apt to be the rule rather than exception.

Within four days the capricious micro-organisms had traced an arc across the city of Boston and hit the Navy Radio School in Cambridge. By the end of the first week in September, Boston was luckless host to two thousand Navy cases of influenza.

Captain Blackwood's once neat, peaceful command had been turned into a vast contagion ward. Tents were being pitched on the hospital lawns to handle the overflow of patients, as the number of sick approached twice the bed space of Chelsea Naval Hospital.

The concerns of a few short days ago, especially Captain Blackwood's desire for a new official automobile, seemed inconsequential and even frivolous. Any sort of vehicle, engine- or horse-propelled, was welcomed to transport the mounting multitudes of the stricken.

This same week, a liner arrived in New York from France. Two of the passengers, Italians, had died of flu, or possibly pneumonia, during the voyage; at least twenty-five had been stricken.

Claude A. Wales, representing the Locomotive Company of Bridgeport, Connecticut, reported that the disease had been prevalent among the longshoremen at the port of embarkation. "I have had the old-fashioned grippe and tropical fever," Wales asserted, "but nothing that hit me quite so hard as the new Spanish influenza. It gives its victims a bad headache and a worse grouch." The representatives of the locomotive manufacturer were able to walk down the gangplank, although stretchers were required to remove other patients to quarantine.

New York, however, was neither anticipating an epidemic nor braced for one. Dr. Royal Copeland, the health commissioner, pointed out that there were very few cases of pneumonia, "an absolutely reliable index of the possible prevalence of the disease." Nonetheless, East Coast ports down to Florida were being challenged by the flu. Navy buildings and patrol vessels were the first to come under fire from the advance pickets of the epidemic. Thirty seamen from the Brooklyn Navy Yard, for example, were admitted on one morning to Bellevue Hospital. The ailment of all was diagnosed as influenza. Soldiers returning on transports also were spottily infected.

In Boston, the *Daily Globe* announced: GRIPPE MAKING GREAT HEADWAY. Calling for nurses and volunteers, Dr. William C. Woodward, Boston's health commissioner, revealed that at least three thousand persons were ill with Spanish influenza. In a twenty-four-hour period there had been forty deaths.

The whole city was rallying, even as it had those long-ago days of Lexington, Concord and Bunker Hill. The overtaxed City Hospital was closed to visitors. At Corey Hill, Brookline, health department workers and soldiers pitched a tent hospital. Its makeshift character was underscored by the use of fire hydrants as water taps.These quick-to-erect emergency hospitals appeared to be an answer to other communities' epidemic needs. Haverhill and Lawrence planned to follow Brookline's lead.

By now a total of thirty-two patients had died at Chelsea Naval Hospital, where admissions continued to average 152 a day. Captain Blackwood, who had lost one of his own staff, Surgeon Harold G. Porter, nonetheless described the Navy's infestation as "comparatively small."

As though it had consolidated its headquarters in Boston, the rampaging invader continued to sally out in all directions: to Portsmouth, New Hampshire; to Newport, Rhode Island; to Camp Devens near Ayer, Massachusetts. At Devens, wrested out of the forests only a year previously to train the Yankee Division, staccato commands were fewer, in testimony to depleting ranks. The entire camp of 41,000 troops was placed under quarantine.

Dr. William Henry Welch, eminent Johns Hopkins University pathologist, whose career had spanned nearly half a century, was summoned to the stricken camp. A younger colleague, accompanying him on his rounds, reported on the spectacle, made all the more dismal by a cold, steady rain: "There was a continuous line of men coming in from the various barracks, carrying their blankets, many of the men looking extremely ill . . . there were not enough nurses, and the poor boys were putting themselves to bed on cots, which overflowed out of the wards on the porches."

Some were cyanotic, blue in color, from lung congestion. The soldiers presented a pitiful sight in their remaining moments of life and in death. Dr. Welch himself was awed at the results of the autopsies. "This must be some new kind of infection or plague," he declared.

Dr. Victor C. Vaughan, sixty-one-year-old Assistant Surgeon General and head of the Army's communicable diseases section, received urgent instructions: "You will proceed immediately to Devens. The Spanish influenza has struck that camp." It was not an easy order to obey. Just returned from an inspection trip to Southern training areas, Dr. Vaughan himself was ailing with at least a bad cold.

Brockton, an important manufacturing city of fifty thousand souls, was singled out, mysteriously enough, for disproportionate fury from the disease. There, fifteen hundred persons were already ill. Mayor William L. Gleason, forced by circumstance to become a twentieth-century Minute Man, was galvanized into a whirlwind of action. He organized committees of doctors, nurses and volunteer helpers. He established kitchens, and day nurseries for the children of sick parents. He reopened the old Goddard Hospital which had just been replaced by a new structure. He mobilized the Boy Scouts, holding them in readiness to carry messages and run errands, closed the schools, theaters and all public places of gathering. The city was under an almost — but not quite — hermetically tight quarantine, "buttoned up" for the duration.

"It still isn't enough," adjured Dr. Carl Holmberg, chairman of Brockton's board of health. But he had to admit he did not know what else to suggest to his friend Bill Gleason. As he had confided to a student nurse at the Brockton Hospital, Greta Lindblad, whom he was courting, battling the influenza was like "fighting with a ghost." One could never come to grips with this adversary.

Doctors in Seattle as well as in New Orleans were already echoing Dr. Holmberg's frustration. Again, however, Boston had been the focus of infection, the outbreaks in the Puget Sound area and along the Gulf Coast having been traced to a troop train in the former case and a ship in the latter. Both had originated in the Massachusetts capital.

"The rapidity of the spread of influenza throughout a country is only limited by the rapidity of the means of transportation," explained Dr. Hermann M. Biggs, pathologist and New York State Public Health Commissioner. "The disease is carried from place to place by persons, not things. Its rapid extension is due to its great infectivity, the short period of incubation, usually two days or less, the mild or missed cases, and the absence of proper precautionary measures."

A phenomenon in transportation and incubation had happened aboard the transport *Olympic*. Within a few days of her docking in Southampton, England, twenty-three hundred of the American troops who had been aboard her contracted flu, and 119 succumbed. In the closely packed troop compartments the disease had blazed like dry kindling. Once it was burning, there had been no stopping it.

3

WHAT WAS INFLUENZA? Where did it come from? What could be done about it? Professional and amateur, frustrated by shadow-boxing with a shadow which demonstrably hit back, and hit hard, posed these questions. The State of Virginia printed them into a catechism for its citizens:

Q. What is influenza?
A. Influenza is a disease which starts with a chill or chilly feelings, makes a person very feverish and weak, and causes a cough, sore throat, and much aching.
Q. What other names are there for this disease?
A. Grippe, the flu, and Spanish influenza.
Q. Is influenza a new disease?
A. No.
Q. What causes influenza?
A. A tiny living poisonous plant called the germ of influenza.
Q. Has this epidemic of influenza been altogether a curse?
A. No, if we learn from this experience the lessons that we should learn, it will mean a blessing in disguise, for it will cause the reduction of the sick and death rate from many other diseases.

The United States Navy Surgeon General, more definite, published a bulletin for his physicians:

> A sudden onset, with malaise and weakness, leading in a few hours to prostration out of proportion to other clinical manifestations; the prominence of headache, particularly the so-called post-orbital headache; muscular pains, sharp rise in temperature to 101 or 102 degrees or even higher, and leucopenia appear to be the principal guides to recognition of the true case of influenza.

Surgeon General Rupert Blue, of the United States Public Health Service, sent out a communiqué which could be readily understood by almost anyone:

> In most cases, a person taken sick with influenza feels sick rather suddenly. He feels weak, has pains in the eyes, ears, head or back, abdomen, etc., and may be sore all over. Many patients feel dizzy. . . .
>
> In appearance one is struck by the fact that the patient looks sick. . . . Ordinarily the fever lasts from three to four days and the patient recovers. But while the proportion of deaths is usually low, in some places the outbreak is severe and deaths are numerous. When death occurs, it is usually the result of the development of a pneumonia or of some other complication.
>
> Occasionally there are nervous symptoms; sometimes, but not always, the eyes and the air passages of the nose and throat are affected; there may be gastrointestinal disturbances. The bacteriology is not definitely established. Often the Pfeiffer bacillus can be isolated. The most fatal complication is pneumonia. In most instances the patient recovers in three or four days, but is entirely incapacitated for duty while the attack is at its height. In a certain proportion of cases convalescence is slow. Relapses may occur.

There were almost as many theories as there were medical men, not only as to what influenza was, but as to how it should be combated.

"Influenza," declared Dr. Louis Dechmann, of Seattle, "is a negative disease. I am of the opinion that it would be more accurate to name this disease *panasthenia:* a general loss of vitality." As treatment, he suggested an abdomen pack of towels soaked in hot vinegar: "The acetic acid of vinegar is absorbed through the pores and transformed into acetate, which will prevent coagulation of the blood." One's diet, prescribed Dr. Dechmann, should be egg punch, custard, graham crackers and milk toast. If the vinegar packs or menu did not produce results he suggested the patient telephone him at "Ballard 2274."

Without attempting to explain the nature or family tree of Spanish influenza, Lieutenant Colonel Philip S. Doane, head of the health and sanitation section of the Emergency Fleet Corporation, offered his opinion on how the deadly organisms had arrived in America.

"We know," he declared, "that men have been ashore from German submarine boats. It would be quite easy for one of these German agents to turn loose Spanish influenza germs in a theater or some place where large numbers of persons are assembled."

That bacteria could be sown like grass seed did not seem too far-fetched to Colonel Doane or to others. Many heeded a rumor that a hidden German laboratory in Chevy Chase, Maryland, bordering the national capital, was the dissemination point for a devil's brew of influenza.

On Thursday, September 19, Assistant Secretary of the Navy Franklin D. Roosevelt landed in New York following a two-months tour of the front lines and overseas naval bases. The handsome thirty-six-year-old next in command to Josephus Daniels was carried from the transport *Leviathan* and into a waiting ambulance. Seriously ill with the flu, he was taken to the home of his mother, Mrs. James Roosevelt, at 47 East 65th

Street. Dr. A. H. Ely, the family physician, was summoned.

By now, Massachusetts had organized a State Emergency Health Committee as life and industry of the Bay State slowed. The Stock Exchange went on a half-day in Boston, theaters were closed and athletic contests canceled. Liberty Loan parades were postponed.

Schools, however, presented their own special challenge: whether to close them or not. In tenement areas, children were in a cleaner, less crowded environment at classes than at home, irrespective of epidemic. On the other hand, school structures were needed for other purposes in some hard-hit neighborhoods. An early compromise, putting masks on the children in class, proved chaotic. The unnatural face covering was too distracting. Ultimately, whether to close schools or leave them open became a matter for the individual community or section of a large city to determine.

In Quincy, Massachusetts, the sound of the riveter, which had beaten its victory tattoo in the shipyards, was muted as worker after worker sickened. Three men, perhaps seeking medical help, dropped dead on Quincy's sidewalks on a single afternoon.

A churchless Sunday, September 22, was proclaimed for Boston. In this apprehensive city, with a daily death toll from the flu alarmingly close to the two hundred mark, the ban was unnecessary, even for the devout. An ostrich complex was laying hold upon the populace. If one clung to home, closed doors, windows and spoke to no one, the terrible plague just *might* be avoided. With such a philosophy of self-deception, male and female parroted a poem—

> I had a little bird
> Its name was Enza,
> I opened the window
> And in-flu-Enza —

which held an incongruous appeal even for those of better-than-average intellect or education. The doggerel, by the same token, made as much sense as a cartoon depicting a cloaked figure labeled "Spanish Influenza" muttering "*Caramba!*" In the next sequence, after his disguise had been snatched off, he was growling, "Heck! I'm diskivered!" He had turned out to be merely "Old Man Grippe."

Surgeon General Blue, of the United States Public Health Service, saw nothing funny about "Old Man Grippe." He dictated an urgent bulletin on the dangers of incorrectly diagnosing flu:

> It is important that influenza be kept out of the camps as far as practicable. To this end it must be recognized as a disease which is distinct and separate from the so-called "cold, bronchitis, laryngitis, coryza, or rhinitis and fever type" which are continually with us and from time to time become prevalent.

Unhappily, influenza was already in the camps. All the bulletins, the gauze masks and, indeed, all the king's horses or men could not keep the infection out.

On September 25, Margaret Sullivan, a nurse, and fifty soldiers died at Camp Devens, where 1543 new cases in the past twenty-four hours had skyrocketed the total number of soldiers afflicted to more than five thousand. One quarter the muster strength, two thousand men, were taken sick on the same day at Camp Beauregard, Louisiana. Camp Dix, New Jersey, was registering a thousand new cases daily, while the flu was just invading Camps Lee and Eustis in Virginia, Sherman in Ohio, and Kearny in California.

At Camp Funston, the flu finally completed a round trip. It had come home. Lieutenant Colonel Glenn I. Jones, who had succeeded Dr. Schreiner as camp surgeon, prepared for the worst.

The commanding officer of Fort St. Philip, on the Mississippi River, just below New Orleans, clamped a quarantine on the small post, allowing no one to leave or enter.

At the same time, the captain of the United States Naval Training Station on Goat Island, in San Francisco Bay, resolved that he too could keep the disease out. All officers and men attached to the station were summoned back from the mainland. Guards were placed at the docks with orders to shoot to kill anyone embarking or disembarking without authorization. Crewmen of ferries, tugs and supply launches were kept, at gun point, on the far decks of their craft.

An absolute quarantine was imposed upon the encampment of four thousand souls. Every man was inoculated with what vaccine was available. Drinking fountains were sterilized hourly with blow torches, telephones doused with alcohol, and muslin coverings were provided for every cot. New trainees, or "boots," were ordered to march and, in fact, exist constantly twenty feet from one another. Their throats were swabbed with silver nitrate, their noses sprayed with a slightly less abrasive solution. For a week before their training commenced they were sealed off from others.

No liberty was allowed to San Francisco or Oakland. What made this separation especially vexatious for the families left on the mainland was the truth that there was little influenza in the Bay area. To wives and to not a few sweethearts, suddenly condemned to a monastic existence, the action of the training station seemed hysterical. Equally dismayed were the waterfront's "gull girls," now separated from their clientele. Nor could they think of any more auspicious roosting places.

Yet not everyone regarded the flu with alarm, and not everyone contemplated its treatment with despair. Many with no background in the sciences whatsoever believed they had divined the secrets of infection.

35

I wish to tell you how I and my daughter were cured of the influenza without a doctor [wrote Mrs. Katerina Poskocil, of East 139th Street in Cleveland's "Little Czechoslovakia," to Secretary of War Newton D. Baker]. Cut up two large onions and add to them rye flour, until there is formed a thick paste; make it into a cake, wrap it in a thin white cloth and apply it to the chest. . . . In bed I put to my lips a wet towel and at night I was so fine. The next day the influenza was gone. The onions drive away infection.

A Boston firm offered "Cetolates Tablets," for which it claimed that "one tablet three or four times daily may prevent serious attack" of influenza.

Officials in positions of trust and responsibility could not, however, rely upon poultices or pills. Among their number was Lieutenant Governor Calvin Coolidge, of Massachusetts, who telegraphed President Wilson on September 27 that his state was "urgently in need of additional doctors and nurses." He addressed similar appeals to the Governors of Vermont, Maine and Rhode Island and to the Mayor of Toronto, Canada. New Hampshire and Connecticut were themselves too seriously infected to be expected to help their neighbor. In New Hampshire, Governor Henry W. Keyes was sick. The coastal areas of Connecticut had been buffeted by the bacteria as they might by winter gales. At New London, the Navy Submarine Base was partially crippled by the epidemic.

The effect on the nation's military effort was becoming even more pronounced. The *New York Times* announced in a one-column headline on September 27:

INFLUENZA STOPS

FLOW TO THE CAMPS

OF DRAFTED MEN

Provost Marshal Enoch Crowder, who had been devoting much of his attention to "draft dodgers" and "slackers," now focused on this newer and conceivably greater menace. His reaction was characteristically decisive. He canceled a call for 142,000 men due to report to the Army the following week. There was ample reason for his drastic measure. With more than 35,000 already ill in the camps, 6139 new cases had been recorded in the past twenty-four hours.

Such a suspension, unavoidable as it was, came at a time when General Pershing was cabling for fresh troops. Most recently, he had advised the War Department: "Attention is especially invited to the very great shortage in arrivals of replacements heretofore requested. Situation with reference to replacements is now very acute." Already the Commander-in-Chief was resorting to "skeletonizing" newly disembarked divisions and distributing officers and men among other units in the front lines. But even this could not be done much longer. The source at home had dried.

Secretary of the Interior Franklin K. Lane requested that the United States Public Health Service be granted a million dollars in federal funds to increase its assistance to the nation. Surgeon General Blue would be authorized to employ 1085 additional physicians and 703 nurses. Yet the money and the authorization were of secondary importance. Where would Dr. Blue find doctors and nurses? The insatiable appetite of war had drawn much of the nation's qualified medical personnel overseas. The Army alone had 17,000 physicians in uniform.

It had become a fight against time and disease even to move additional components of the A.E.F. to France. The U.S.S. *Virginia*, as but one example, was in Boston minus an executive officer. Lieutenant Commander Hugh Brown, a big, friendly man, impatient for such an assignment ever since war had been declared, was hurrying from the Naval Academy to assume the second commanding position aboard the big battleship. When he arrived at South Station, however, this last week in September, Commander Brown was fiery with fever. Nearly delirious, he was taken to Chelsea Naval Hospital. The U.S.S. *Virginia*, leaving seventy-five of its men behind in the same hospital, put out into the submarine-infested wastes of the Atlantic without an executive officer. Commander Brown was dead.

But the war could not wait. On September 28, the 57th Pioneer Infantry Regiment of the 31st Division had finished months of training. The jaunty Vermonters had an important date this bright, crisp Saturday evening — with the transport *Leviathan*, warped, steam up, at Hoboken.

One of the battalions of the regiment, which had a total strength of 3153 men and 100 officers, started from a staging area in Yonkers, New York. The unit, under the leadership of Colonel E. W. Gibson of Brattleboro, would march through Yonkers to a ferry and would then steam down the Hudson to the giant of the seas, which before its seizure by the United States had been the German *Vaterland*.

We had proceeded but a short distance [reported Colonel Gibson] when it was discovered that the men were falling out of ranks, unable to keep up.

The attention of the commanding officer was called to the situation. The column was halted and the camp surgeon was summoned. The examination showed that the dreaded influenza had hit us. Although many men had fallen out, we were ordered to resume the march. We went forward up and up over the winding moonlit road leading to Alpine Landing on the Hudson where ferry boats were waiting to take us to Hoboken.

The victims of the epidemic fell on either side of the road, unable to carry their heavy packs. Some threw their equipment away and with determination tried to keep up with their comrades. Army trucks and ambulances, following, picked up those who had fallen and took them back to the camp hospital. How many men or how much equipment was lost on that march?

On board the transport, men continued to be stricken and 100 of these were taken off and returned to shore before sailing. . . . We had on board 9033 officers and men and about 200 Army nurses on their way to hospitals in France.

It was a mixed sailing on this, the world's largest vessel: the 323rd Signal Battalion, three pontoon outfits, three companies of Negro sappers, together with the medical group which represented replacements for two base hospitals.

Major General LeRoy S. Lyon, commander of the 31st Division, was also aware they had embarked on an inauspicious note. The veteran general did not have to be a medical officer to sense that. Captain W. W. Phelps, skipper of the massive and unwieldy liner, was somewhat more phlegmatic. This was but another Atlantic crossing he must make, and was listed on his manifests as "Voyage No. 9."

4

WHILE Spanish influenza shared the blind wantonness of a forest fire, it also had a seemingly directed venom and often hit where it could be the least substantially withstood.

The infection sought out for its own an increasingly great number of pregnant women, suffocating them as they struggled with their uncustomary, heavy burden. It felled young mothers — thirty-six in one New Hampshire town alone. Fathers under forty years of age were stricken. The stronger the man, seemingly the more rapid was his total physical collapse.

"The husky male," observed Dr. Vaughan, now acting Surgeon General of the Army since Dr. Gorgas had sailed for France, "either made a speedy and rather abrupt recovery or was likely to die. Nature overdoes the resistance, kills the invading organisms too rapidly and sets free such an amount of poison that death occurs . . . Infection, like war, kills the young, vigorous, robust adults."

Boston had spent a cheerless Sunday, this last one in September. Church doors were closed. Their bells were silent, though they might appropriately have tolled in mourning. Motorists, to conserve gasoline and discourage fraternizing, had been ordered to keep their automobiles garaged. Boylston Street was strangely deserted, and no one walked along the banks of the Charles River or watched the lonely swans in the Public Garden. The wind whined across Bunker Hill past a familiar monument around which few children would play or adults pause this Sabbath. Boston could have been the community Defoe referred to when he observed, "What a desolate place the city was at that time."

In Winthrop, police fought to subdue a man crazed with fever. Finally trussed in a straitjacket, he was taken to a hospital. His wife and three children were left abed, too ill to be moved.

In Brockton, the flu raged implacably. Its eight thousand cases, nearly one fifth of the city's population, made a total nearly unparalleled throughout the country. More and more schoolrooms were converted into emergency kitchens. More and more volunteers were sought to feed and care for those who suffered through the illness in their own bedrooms. Age barriers were discarded. Old women and old men appeared behind the soup lines, ladles in hand.

Nurses were arriving from distant states and from Canada to help the almost prostrate city. Among their number were Georgena and Winnifred Flemming, sisters from Londonderry, Nova Scotia. At the Brockton Hospital, where the Flemmings went immediately on duty, there was only one intern, Dr. Helen Haynes. Her male colleagues had gone to war, leaving her with almost around-the-clock responsibilities. There were not only the flu cases, but surgery and the routine assortment of medical ailments, as well as accident patients.

In its cruelty, the disease did not spare doctor or nurse. Two nurses died this Sunday evening at the Brockton Hospital: Gladys Clark, a twenty-five-old student within three weeks of graduation, and Julia Murley, night supervisor. By Monday noon, seventeen patients had succumbed at the same hospital. In alarm, Mayor Gleason called Boston to request the services of state guardsmen.

Harvard opened for its fall term among emergency tents spread on the city's banks. Most of the students kept to the Yard.

Into Gloucester harbor limped the fishing schooner *Athlete*, appearing as though it had sailed from out of the ghostly pages of *The Ancient Mariner*. She was almost a derelict, with her entire crew suddenly, desperately stricken. One member, Frank Poole, was dead. The picturesque fishing port was more effectively checkmated by the epidemic than it had been by winter ice storms and blizzards. Admissions overflowed the modest new Addison Gilbert Hospital, and tents were spread across its broad lawns.

"The whole city is stricken," wrote Lydia Griffin of Gloucester's District Nursing Association. "No help is available from the other cities, and as one of our nurses is also ill with it, it leaves Miss Thomas and Miss Riley to do it all. I called for volunteers who had taken the nursing course and only one was willing to report for duty this afternoon.

"The situation is critical, the hospitals are filled, the doctors are ill . . . We were taken quite unawares."

Half the population of Watkins, New York, was prostrate. The town's largest fraternal organization, the Red Men, offered its hall as a hospital. The high school principal put on an apron and became the emergency institution's chief cook.

The much larger community, San Antonio, Texas, was similarly hit; its military neighbor, Fort Sam Houston, had difficulty finding a bugler well enough to sound Reveille — or, for that matter, Retreat, with all its connotations.

Far to the north, in Michigan's wooded Upper Peninsula, a

slight, wiry woman in Luce County was combating the Spanish influenza in a unique way, dictated by the geography of the area. Annie L. Colon, a public health nurse, accompanied by a doctor, used a handcar to reach her patients. With a red oil lantern on the back of the car and a white one as an imperfect headlight, the two, doctor and nurse, pumped the little vehicle's handbar up and down, up and down. Since Annie was a fraction the weight of the doctor, her problem was one of balance: not to be lifted off her feet every time he pumped down.

It was the only way to penetrate the dense forests into remote lumber camps. With them, over these logging tracks, went as odd a cargo as was ever carried by a handcar: bottles of aspirin, quinine, cough syrup, whiskey, gin and rum, milk cans sloshing with soup, baskets of bread, blankets, bedsheets and even baby toys. If the pair set out at 4 A.M., they could reach the first patients shortly after dawn. It was frosty at that hour, but doctor and nurse worked so unremittingly that they were soon forced to remove overcoats. Nurse Colon wrote to the State Health Department in Lansing:

> We have had a terrible time in this county, losing 100 people or one person out of every 50. . . . I worked with Dr. Perry, our health officer, going to the logging camps, in the hospital, in the homes, wherever the need was greatest at the time. We all worked day and night, hardly taking time to eat.
>
> Some of our patients lived miles back in the woods; not even a road could reach them, but the train could, so we had to go after them in handcars, and so saved many a life.
>
> We hitched a flat-car to a handcar with wire, put a board floor on, mattresses over that, plenty of covers and a canvas to cover the top and break the wind, and we carried the patients 15 or more miles to a decent bed and a chance to live.
>
> We rode 20 and 30 miles at night through the deepest woods and over the roughest roads to camps, and many times

43

we would find 30 or 40 cases, sometimes 10 people all huddled together fully drest in a tiny log cabin, probably all in
two beds and all with fevers over 104°.

On long trips we had one doctor, a driver, one helper and
myself, and we just worked and instructed and showed those
among them who could help what to do, when we had to
leave . . . Everybody worked hard and long with unselfish
spirit.

Whiskey proved effective medicine for the lumberjacks.
Bottle in hand, they curled up under their blankets, confident
of being cured.

Newberry, the county seat, was a ghost town. Even the hotel
had been turned into a hospital. The lack, as elsewhere, was of
doctors and nurses. One social worker who had been dispatched from Lansing aroused the ire of citizens who charged
that he had done "little except give the local people hell for
not making out daily reports when they were already dead on
their feet." Across Lake Michigan, taps had been sounded for
489 sailors at the Great Lakes Naval Training Station, though
the doctors believed the rate was downward. Nonetheless, one
fourth of the 45,000 men stationed there were ill.

In Chicago, an Influenza Commission had just been created.
The city's West Side Hospital was attacked with disproportionate severity. At least twenty-five of its nurses were now bedded
with the fever. Dr. C. St. Clair Drake, Director of the State
Department of Public Health, ordered all hospital attendants
to wear masks. He hoped this expedient would insure against
repetition of the West Side Hospital's crippling experience.

In suburban Glencoe and Winnetka, soldiers of the Home
Guard patrolled closed schoolyards, as well as the padlocked
saloons and movie theaters. Bulletins apprising the citizenry of
the rapidly changing situation were printed each morning and
distributed by the Boy Scouts.

How to stem this bacterial tide? Advice poured into the Surgeon General's office, to the White House, to the Public Health Service, to Congressmen and to every daily or weekly newspaper in America.

> Take two pieces of flannel each 12 x 14 inches [wrote J. J. C. Elliott, Former Superintendent of the Methodist Hospital in Los Angeles], sprinkle over one or two of the small packages of wormwood purchased from drug stores usually for ten cents. Lay the other over the sprinkled wormwood and stitch around the edges and quilt them across each way so the wormwood may be held evenly over the entire bag. Place one of these bags in vinegar as hot as it can possibly be wrung from the vinegar and place the bag over the chest of the patient, covering the flannel with bed clothing.

In Seattle, policemen were ordered to wear masks at all times. Citizens must don them in order to ride the public transit. Oregon was confronted with medical challenges for which there was little precedent: sick sheepherders. It was bewildering to rationalize how the flu had sought them out in their isolation, and it was yet more vexing to treat them. A public health nurse at Denio, Oregon, wrote headquarters of her special problems:

> Our patients are mostly families of sheepherders; they live in miserable cabins scattered in most inaccessible places, a house to a hill and each hill from 12 to 15 miles apart. There is no food, no bedding and absolutely no conception of the first principles of hygiene, sanitation or nursing care.
>
> I have taken over the hotel as a hospital and the Big Boss, who employs the sheepherders, is having all who are not too ill to be moved brought in here.
>
> The men are willing, some are intelligent, but most are sick, and if it were not for the grit and brains of the nurses who have been working here before and for the women of the community, God help us!
>
> I am working by fits and starts, as I can snatch a minute off to jot down our needs, hoping that the situation may be

clear to you and that you will be able to get us some supplies before we get snowed in for the winter. Our greatest need (next to fruit and malted milk) is feeding cups and drinking tubes, also need lots of gauze and cheesecloth and cotton for pneumonia jackets; also rubber sheeting and quantities of old rags, to be used and burned, also gallons of formaldehyde, if we are to stamp out the disease; everything is thrown on the ground and will thaw out next spring and release all these germs again if we do not take precautions against it.

At Norfolk, Virginia, five thousand sailors were ill. In West Virginia, uncounted thousands of coal miners were absent from the shafts. Coal shortages, at a time when warmth was needed, were coupled with rocketing prices, and there was no ceiling in sight.

Three thousand residents of Wilmington, Delaware, were sick. Delaware College, at nearby Newark, sent its few well students home and sealed the campus.

America was shaken. Many who could scarcely remember the last time they went to church now belatedly and passionately beseeched the Lord to spare them. For some there was a lurking suspicion that Judgment Day was near, man having been called to account for his sin and wickedness. "Epidemics," opined the *New York Evening Post*, "are the punishment which nature inflicts for the violation of her laws and ordinances." Others, perhaps mindful of September's last hours, turned to poetry. They would have found these doleful lines of Edgar Allan Poe peculiarly appropriate:

> The skies they were ashen and sober;
> The leaves they were crispèd and sere —
> The leaves they were withering and sere;
> It was night in the lonesome October . . .

5

OCTOBER ARRIVED amidst a scurry of summer's brittling leaves, and many medical research men turned their attention to this will-o'-the-wisp that killed so wantonly. How could they seek out and ultimately destroy an enemy that was as unknown as life itself? It could be living matter, of a microscopic character, as bacteria are; it could be of the enigmatical virus species, which posed its own riddle; or it could be an inert but destructive blob of protein.

This maniac of the microbe world was hunted with exhaustive dedication at laboratories of the Rockefeller Institute in New York. The head of the Department of Pathology and Bacteriology, Dr. Simon Flexner, had requested a meticulous researcher, Dr. Martha Wollstein, to subordinate every other duty and interest to the quest for the elusive mass-murderer.

A modest and retiring woman of fifty, Dr. Wollstein was at home nowhere with more familiarity or sense of belonging as in the world of medical bacteriology. The inspiration and the poetry in her life were the tracts of the medical immortals and others who had not quite reached immortality.

In her new project, her first task was to resolve the findings of Dr. Richard Pfeiffer, whose word was a creed to many of Dr. Wollstein's clinical faith: *"Ich hatte mich nach diesen Ergebnissen für berechtigt, diese eben beschriebenen Bacillen als die Erreger der Influenza anzusprechen."*

But was it true? Was he really "justified" in "pronouncing" the bacillus described to be the cause of influenza? Already, like a latter-day Bertillon or a Sherlock Holmes in the narrower sphere of pathology, the serious, tireless Dr. Wollstein was making entries in her own casebook:

> Bacillus influenzae is a frequent invader of the human body, where it either causes or complicates important pathological processes . . . Influenza bacilli isolated from various pathological processes in man differ widely in pathogenic power for animals, especially rabbits . . . Apparently all influenza bacilli belong to one class or race irrespective of origin or virulence.

Among her tools were the accumulating reports on individual manifestations of the current epidemic. Many attested to rarities in medical experience, such as "subcutaneous emphysemas" or inflammations "beginning in the neck and spreading sometimes over the whole body." There were also detailed studies, such as this, from a colleague in London:

> Subsultus tendinum was a marked phenomenon in many cases quite apart from delirium or coma. The patient might be rational enough to be talking about himself and he might even himself call attention to the way he could not keep his legs or arms or back muscles quiet when he wanted to. A leg or an arm or the abdominal muscles or the back would give an involuntary twitch or jerk; or the face or one shoulder, or some other part, the character of the condition approaching in a few instances almost to that of mild chorea. As a rule the prognosis proved bad . . .

Now, New York hospitals were beginning to feel the effects of the epidemic. Interns found the pace of their own duties accelerated out of all proportion. The staff of Presbyterian Hospital was operating normally one afternoon, Dr. Albert Lamb, a resident noted; but the next morning it was "inundated with critically ill cases of influenza." He added:

> On admission most of the early cases were blue as huckleberries. Most of them died. Nearly all were coughing up liquid blood and continued conscious until a short time before death. We had to stand by helpless except for what temporary relief we could give.

Next to Chicago's Hull House, the Henry Street Settlement on New York's lower East Side was the best-known private charity organization in the United States. Its director, Lillian Wald, used to suffering, was nonetheless unprepared for the pleas she had received in the past four days. They were from 467 families reporting cases of influenza and pneumonia.

> The Department of Health and other agencies [Miss Wald wrote to Dr. Copeland, New York's Health Commissioner] are transferring to us cases that come under their notice needing home care, and the number that come from all the agencies and from the people themselves is so great that practically our entire staff is nursing influenza and pneumonia cases. We are also using part-time or married nurses and availing ourselves of all resources and finding great cooperation . . . The demand is excessive and we are not able at all to meet the request for special night work. However, we are doing the very best we can; nobody is hysterical.

Military life at an increasing number of camps had decelerated to a fevered crawl. At Camp Dodge, Iowa, Major J. G. Maxon, surgeon for the 19th Division in formation, was compelled to convert one barracks after another into contagion wards. His problem was a fantastic one: how to fit eight thousand patients into a two thousand-bed hospital?

Camp Meade, Maryland, was counting 1500 new cases every twenty-four hours, a rate which threatened to invalid the entire post. More than 11,000 soldiers — one fourth of the complement — were now too sick readily to distinguish night from day. A report from Camp Pike, Arkansas, was becoming tragically typical:

> Pvt. M., who was drilling in the afternoon, complained of feeling slightly ill. He entered the hospital at 7 o'clock that evening and died next morning at 6. On examination, he showed practically no signs of pneumonia, except a few moist rales which were distributed over both lungs and not confined or isolated to any particular part of the lung. He did however show the following signs of meningitis: headache, depression, hyperesthesia and stiff neck. . . .

The epidemic had caused an atmosphere of depression. The reaction of Lieutenant V. D. Banks of the 12th Infantry Regiment at Camp Fremont, California, was a familiar one as he remarked on "how strangely quiet everything had become." Now, he discovered, the soldiers realized "as never before . . . there was a chaplain." No one could leave the camp, telephone or even write letters home. The canteen was closed, and the troops lined up at its doors while clerks brought wares out to them. "Ambulances," added Lieutenant Banks, "filled with masked patients left almost hourly for the base hospital, and the temporary hospital that had been established at headquarters was crowded."

Colonel Alfred Aloe, the commander, and several other officers were stricken. Prospects of the regiment's ever sailing overseas became increasingly dim, compounding the existing gloom of the soldiers. The 12th Infantry was a proud organization. Its distinguished record included engagements at Gaines's Mill and Gettysburg in the Civil War.

However, it had never faced such an implacable enemy as influenza.

The epidemic dominated national thought, not only in Army

camps. Frustrated, as though they were sparring with an apparition, citizens sought both cause and cure. It mattered not that they were unable to differentiate aspirin from atropine. . . .

"Rinse the mouth with lime water," Joseph Peloquin, of Leavenworth, Kansas, telegraphed the War Department, "inhale hot water and turpentine fumes. This will prevent you getting the Spanish influenza." In the possibility that this prescription did not create immunization, Peloquin was ready with a cure: "Mix a full teaspoonful of ground ginger, a teaspoon of soda, a teaspoonful of sugar in a glass of hot milk, and go to bed." More and more people were going to bed, and nothing — not lime water or turpentine or ginger — would enable them to arise again, ever.

Grief had seemingly seized Boston as its own dwelling place. There 202 persons died on a dark Tuesday, October 1, as H. B. Endicott, executive manager of the Massachusetts Committee on Public Safety, wired to his friend, Secretary of the Navy Daniels:

> As you undoubtedly know, Massachusetts is being hit hard by influenza, so hard that very many cases cannot receive any attention either from doctors or nurses. Anything you can do to help us here in Massachusetts through any forces at your command will be very greatly and gratefully received.

Before nightfall, twenty-five more patients had succumbed in Brockton. Yet creation still struggled to vie with destruction.

While on night duty in the maternity ward," recalled nurse Greta Lindblad at the Brockton Hospital, "a Mrs. Lindquist, a woman in her middle forties, was brought in for her sixth birth. The baby was in a hurry.

"I sent in an emergency for the interne to call but it was past midnight and he had gone to bed. It took a few minutes for him to wake and dress and when he arrived I had already delivered the baby. The patient on hearing my name told me that my mother, an obstetrician, had brought her first child into the world."

Only that afternoon an Italian fruit vendor, nursed back to health, had proposed to Greta, promising her "lots of mon." Unable to resist broad smiles, the nurse frankly told him, "I feel it much wiser to marry for love than fruits and vegetables!"

Nurses throughout the country were presented with varying and often vexing problems by the epidemic. Moving across Pennsylvania, along the old settlers' trail, the influenza had reached Wilkes-Barre.

> For two days [wrote Mrs. Gertrude Williamson, Red Cross nurse in charge of the city's emergency hospital], volunteers worked like beavers, cutting drawsheets, making up the Army cots, scrubbing hatracks to serve as linen shelves and cleaning camp chairs to be used as bedside tables. The Armory was scrubbed from roof to basement and four wards were partitioned off with beaverboard, and lavatories and sinks were installed in the only available rooms.
>
> The Red Cross Canteen Service took entire charge of the basement kitchen and, with a few paid employees, but mostly volunteers, served the nurses, the physicians, the orderlies and the members of the National Guard who were always on duty, besides sending out food, broths mostly, to over 150 families daily, who because of the "flu" had no one well enough to prepare their meals.

These needs, multiplied many times, were transmitted to health and relief agencies in Washington, which struggled to keep up with mountainous orders: morphine, aspirin, quinine, rubbing alcohol, almost a cornucopia of medicine, pajamas, masks, soap, screens, hot water bottles, fly paper, and "pneumonia jackets." The latter heavily padded garments were designed to keep the patient warm even though the room heat might be bordering on the frosty.

Chairman of the Red Cross Henry P. Davison ordered $575,000 in emergency funds set aside and appointed W. Frank Persons as head of a National Committee of Influenza. A well-known social worker, Persons had been director general of civilian relief.

Surgeon General Blue at once appealed to Persons. "The United States Public Health Service has no funds for epidemic control," he explained, adding that nearly all of its nurses were overseas. Congress stepped in. A million dollars, if needed, was authorized for influenza relief. The Army and Navy were requested to supply medical aid, wherever possible, to the civilian population.

Now Washington itself was being cautiously invaded by the disease, which had already taken far heavier toll at two Army forts on its fringes: Camp Meade to the north, A. A. Humphreys to the south.

Louis Brownlow, one of the three District commissioners who presided over this federal city in lieu of a mayor or manager, knew that the flu had already arrived. His two colleagues were in bed with it. A phone call this first Wednesday in October to Dr. William C. Fowler, his health officer, confirmed what he further suspected: at George Washington University Hospital there were forty cases; at Sibley Hospital, where the ailment was labeled simply "la grippe," there were more than twenty. Several doctors and nurses were themselves abed.

Next the efficient Brownlow rang up Dr. R. Ramsay Nevitt, the coroner. "Ramsay," he said, "be prepared for the worst."

Brownlow ordered the shifts of federal offices staggered and limited business hours of stores, except those selling food and drugs, from 10 A.M. to 6 P.M. He also closed schools, theaters, and saloons and forbade public gatherings.

In order to effect the change in the hours of government

workers, beyond the actual jurisdiction of the District commissioners, Brownlow had to seek permission from Secretary of the Treasury William G. McAdoo. President Wilson had shunted off many such extra responsibilities upon the versatile McAdoo, his son-in-law.

"With a characteristic shower of expletives," the Treasury Secretary acceded to Brownlow's request, asking why this had not been done "long before." Brownlow replied that the recommendations, as a means of easing traffic problems, had been on McAdoo's desk "for at least six or seven months." At the same time, Brownlow confronted the already embarrassed and somewhat harassed McAdoo with the intelligence that several dozen of his secretaries, typists and clerks were former nurses. "We've got to get them back in uniform," he curtly informed the Secretary of the Treasury.

One of the factors causing Brownlow to manifest concern, even though the present incidence of Influenza was low, was that the city was jammed with people, perhaps one third above its normal population. Old-time residents took in boarders, temporary housing developments were hammered into being near the Capitol, all to handle the transients the war had brought to Washington.

The Commissioner next ordered nursing centers established in the vacated school buildings, and then requisitioned as an emergency hospital a store at 612 F Street which had been used by the United States Housing Corporation. Dr. James P. Leake, a leading epidemiologist with the United States Public Health Service, was placed in charge. Nearby, a former Western Union office was reopened as a Red Cross recruiting and training station.

Along the more fashionable reaches of 16th Street, in the shadow of the embassies, forty-five society leaders commandeered a garage and cranked into operation a Motor

54

Ambulance Corps. They placed cots along the greasy walls within the garage and prepared for twenty-four-hour duty. While Model T trucks would be the mainstay of the corps, some wealthy women had donated limousines complete with chauffeurs.

By nightfall, twenty-two Washingtonians had died of the flu, and the Motor Ambulance Corps was quickly being put to use. The ladies steered their vehicles into all reaches of the city, from the respectability of Cleveland Park and Chevy Chase to the squalid flats of "banana row," bordering the market district. They carried soup, other nourishment and blankets with them. Some of the sick they fed and made more comfortable. Others they carried out on stretchers and into Dr. Leake's newly established hospital.

Washington was, indeed, mobilized, and with seriousness and determination. One of its physicians, Dr. Noble P. Barnes, expressed this resolve: "Persons at large sneezing and coughing should be treated as a dangerous menace to the community, properly fined, imprisoned and compelled to wear masks until they are educated out of that 'Gesundheit!' and 'God bless you!' rot."

To some the greatest personal tragedy was the padlocking of places of entertainment, theaters and bars. In war this meant that many people would be left alone with their fears . . . Washington had been movie and vaudeville-conscious. Now arc lights sputtered out at 10:30 that evening in several dozen projectors. Many big names went off the marquees: William S. Hart in *The Border Wireless;* Will Rogers in *Laughing Bill Hyde;* Dorothy Gish in *Battling Jane.* At the National Burlesque, Flo-Flo and her "Perfect 36" chorus would frolic no more in *Frolics of the Night.*

This was also trying to Woodrow Wilson, whose principal diversion had been vaudeville. At least one evening a week, the scholarly President with the pince-nez used to be seen striding across Executive Place to B. F. Keith's Theater, two blocks distant.

Somewhere en route to Washington, Julia Sanderson and Joseph Cawthorn, booked for *The Canary*, received a telegram. They would travel no farther. *The Canary* was caged for the duration. So were thousands of actors and actresses, trapped at one- or seven-night stands throughout the nation.

6

DR. B. F. ROYER, Health Commissioner for Pennsylvania, took a drastic step at the end of this first week in October. He had checked with the forty-six hospitals in greater Philadelphia and Camden and their clinics and found that there were at least 75,000 cases of flu. For a city of 1,800,000 the proportion might not have appeared great. Yet Dr. Royer had sufficient experience in epidemiology to know the tendency of infectious waves to double, redouble and keep redoubling in volume. He had also visited the steel and coal communities of Bethlehem and Reading and telephoned to his assistants in Pittsburgh. To his alarm, he learned that absenteeism was increasing far beyond safe levels. He was convinced that he must institute a statewide ban with the same objectives that Commissioner Brownlow had just effected in Washington. And this is exactly what Dr. Royer did.

In Philadelphia, the state's major city, theaters, saloons, schools, churches and, in fact, all places of public meeting were closed. The rules that were thus promulgated were distressingly reminiscent of Defoe's detailed imaginings:

That all plays, bear-baitings, games, singing of ballads, buckler-play, or such-like causes of assemblies of people be utterly prohibited, and the parties offending severely punished by every alderman in his ward.

That all public feastings, and particularly by the companies of this city, and dinners at taverns, ale-houses, and other places of common entertainment, be forborne till further order and allowance; and that the money thereby spared be preserved and employed for the benefit and relief of the poor visited with the infection.

That disorderly tippling in taverns, ale-houses, coffeehouses, and cellars be severely looked into, as the common sin of this time and the greatest occasion of dispersing the plague.

The situation in Philadelphia alone was critical, with a thousand of its physicians and nearly the same number of nurses absent in military service. As Dr. Royer pointed out, this represented "an abnormal shortage of medical aid" and magnified the city's potential dangers. Dr. A. A. Cairns, president of Philadelphia's board of health, published a plea for retired nurses and doctors. Age mattered not a whit, or even agility, he asserted — just so they remembered "even a little" of their profession.

As part of the hasty mobilization, the Philadelphia Council of National Defense set up a telephone switchboard at the Strawbridge and Clothier department store. Anyone desiring soup, clothing, a nurse, doctor or — an undertaker — had but to call "Filbert 100." On Arch Street, near the City Hall, a Catholic literary society, the Philopatrian Club, stretched sheets across tiers of dusty shelves and infrequently read volumes. Mahogany center tables were replaced with cots. The old brick structure had been converted into a flu hospital. Dr. Henry A. Strecker, a prominent Philadelphia physician and also Philopatrian, volunteered to serve as the club's medical director. The Sisters of St. Joseph would furnish the nursing. Archbishop Daugherty had exempted the order from vows which prohibited the Sisters from entering private homes. Now the skilled holy women could serve as special nurses anywhere needed, irrespective of the denomination of the person or institution.

The flu, in many respects, was proving a leveler, even as war itself. It crossed social and religious boundaries with equal facility. St. John's Day Nursery and St. Stephen's Episcopal Church were also preparing wards for the admission of anyone stricken with the flu: Protestant, Catholic, Jew, Mohammedan or even the militant atheist.

These measures were being instituted none too soon. The flu had already invaded the city that Benjamin Franklin once knew and loved, from Rittenhouse Square, where the elm and linden leaves lay brown and golden on the walks, past Fairmont Park, to the litter-strewn reaches of upper Broad Street. Yet . . . in one odorous flat on the latter thoroughfare, a social worker found a woman, sick in bed near the lifeless body of her husband; she had not only delivered twins without assistance, but had survived, fevered as she was, on the nourishment of one apple.

In Washington the machinery of government continued to turn more slowly. Herbert Hoover's Food Administration was recording 50 per cent illness among its personnel. Mrs. Hoover had gone to work as a volunteer health aide. Transportation was seriously crippled, with 260 street car motormen and other employees of the transportation company ill.

Ten miles down the Potomac River, in the sleepy community of Alexandria where George Washington had once worshiped and his wife Martha had done the family marketing, civic rigor mortis was being approached. Only two doctors remained mobile. In the morning, they left Warfield's Drug Store, carrying thousands of terpin hydrate and atropin capsules plus all the whiskey they could obtain by prescription or other means. Thus burdened, they commenced their rounds, dispensing "flu cures" from house to shanty and even to the numerous river boats moored in the creeks which led into the Potomac. Overshadowed by the greater needs in Washington, Alexandria had to be content with only these two champions of communal health.

At neighboring Camp Humphreys in Virginia, Lieutenant Colonel Charles E. Doerr, newly promoted to command of the hospital, succumbed. He had shrugged off the suggestions of other doctors that he take to bed, fighting a mounting fever to care for nearly five thousand ill soldiers at this engineers' replacement center. There was not a physician available to escort the surgeon's body home to Kentucky. Overworked Army doctors, in fact, were asking for help from Camp Meade.

The flu was pummeling more and more Army camps. At Camp Grant, near Rockford, Illinois, 10,713 soldiers, one third of the complement, were sick. The rate at least vied with that of Camp Meade and Camp Devens, which hitherto had been considered the worst pestilence spots in the nation.

> The rapidity with which cases developed during the height of the epidemic [read the report from the Camp Grant surgeon's office] promptly flooded the base hospital, and it became necessary to equip various infirmaries throughout the camp to receive patients. When the housing space in the infirmaries was filled, one or more contiguous barracks in each area were assigned for the reception of patients. All mild cases were received in the infirmary wards, and if the cases became more severe, they were transferred at once to the base hospital. These wards were also used for the reception of convalescents returned from the base hospital, who were held for about a week for observation before being returned to duty.

Post-infection heart complications, such as tachycardia, were already being diagnosed by the surgeons, who also noted one phenomenon: none of the contingent of German prisoners at the camp had been infected.

There were nearly one thousand cases at Camp Funston, where the flu had fragmented the 10th Division in the initial stage of formation. With 60 per cent of its strength invalided, the 30th Machine Gun Battalion virtually went out of existence except as an entry on Army Task Organization lists. The hospital was rapidly filling, once more. Dr. Jones and his chief nurse, Elizabeth Harding, started looking around for areas of expansion.

The West Coast was more spottily infected. At San Jose, California, the State Normal School was being operated as a convalescent hospital. Townspeople donated food and clothing, while the faculty, wearing masks, worked in the diet kitchen. "I wish I could do more," confided a motherly-looking woman to Miss Charlotte A. Morton, director of the school's household arts department. The elderly lady had carried a crib full of potatoes to the school. One young doctor had organized the hospital, aided by a trained nurse and seventy-five untrained volunteers.

At Modesto, California, an expedient adopted to continue the students' homework, even though the schools were closed, held promise for future procedure. Assignments were published in the newspapers. The pupils either mailed their completed lessons to the teachers or, swathed in face masks, brought them to the school for brief discussion. It might, teachers speculated, evolve into permanent "correspondence courses."

In Chicago, Health Commissioner Dr. John Dill Robertson, just returned from Washington, declared, "I believe this epidemic insofar as Chicago is concerned, will pass within five weeks." Ninety-two persons had died in the city from flu and pneumonia in the past twenty-four hours. He asked the city council for $100,000 as a special influenza fund and reemphasized his stand on "openfaced sneezers" and spitters. "Arrest thousands, if necessary, to stop sneezing in public!" he ordered the police department. His fury did not cease there, as he added, "If I find evidence against any greedy landlord having turned off the heat and the tenant dies, I shall ask the state's attorney to indict him on a charge of murder."

The Red Cross issued an appeal for those who had been exposed to any nurse's training whatsoever. They should telephone "Randolph 7480."

Plans of many persons in many, many places were completely disrupted. Newspapers were filled with announcements of cancellations. In Cleveland, for example, the Quest Club would not gather, as scheduled, at the home of Mrs. W. E. Foote, of 1246 East 102nd Street. The members would have to bide their curiosity until after the epidemic for an answer to the topic "For what do I first look when I open my newspaper?" Few readers sought out stories on the flu epidemic. Those who did found the most meager information. There was, apparently, a tacit conspiracy among the nation's editors to hush-hush the ever-mounting ravages, as though they hoped that if they did not notice, the infection would go away. But the infection did not go away. In New York, the scourge was gaining speed with reckless headway. The death rate was now exceeding one hundred a day. At Bellevue Hospital, it was not entirely infrequent for a patient at one end of a ward to call hoarsely for a nurse at the other — and die by the time she reached the bedside. In the children's ward, youngsters were being packed in three to a bed. Neither medical care nor facilities could keep pace with the meteoric character of Spanish influenza.

Across the bay, on Staten Island, the micro-organisms were also busy with deadly seriousness. The shipyards were reporting 40 per cent absenteeism. Rates of attrition were nearly as high in other East Coast and also Gulf Coast yards. Officials had cause for concern. "Ship production," announced Charles M. Schwab, Director General of the Emergency Fleet Corporation, "is imperiled by the flu." And in Brest the *Leviathan,* from which the 57th Pioneer Infantry had disembarked, had become a pest ship. The infestation which had attacked the regiment as it marched through Yonkers had not relaxed its strangle hold.

> The ship was packed [wrote Colonel Gibson], conditions were such that the influenza bacillus could breed and multiply with extraordinary swiftness. We went much of the way without convoy. The U-boat menace made it necessary to keep every port hole closed at night, and the air below decks where the men slept was hot and heavy. The number of sick increased rapidly. Washington was apprised of the situation, but the call for men for the Allied armies was so great that we must go on at any cost. The sick bay became overcrowded and it became necessary to evacuate the greater portion of Deck E and turn that into sick quarters. Doctors and nurses were stricken. Every available doctor and nurse was utilized to the limit of endurance.
>
> The conditions during the night cannot be visualized by anyone who had not actually seen them . . . groans and cries of the terrified added to the confusion of the applicants clamoring for treatment, and altogether a true inferno reigned supreme.

The presence on board of the two hundred Army nurses saved Voyage No. 9 from being complete calamity. Nonetheless, the men were still not rid of their nemesis after they had disembarked. "All who were able to march," Gibson continued, "were moved to the mud flats beyond the Pontanezzan Barracks. Several hundred of the men never reached camp or their organizations. They were picked up by the YMCA or KC men or by Army ambulances and taken to hospitals as soon as they were able to walk. . . . Nearly 200 of the regiment were buried in the American cemetery at Lambezellec."

General Pershing, whose A.E.F. was apparently winning the vast battle of the Meuse-Argonne, now took notice of influenza as he reported:

> Influenza in the Army had assumed very serious proportions, over 16,000 cases additional having been reported during the week ending October 5th. Large numbers of cases were brought in by our troop ships. The total number of cases of influenza treated in hospitals was nearly 70,000, of whom many developed a grave form of pneumonia. The death rate from influenza rose to 32 per cent of cases for the A.E.F. and was as high as 80 per cent in some groups.

And in London, Dr. French was again reporting on the development of the epidemic:

> . . . in the middle of severe cases one saw the constantly repeated picture of a dreadful malady which few physicians had seen the like before . . . Even the mildest cases had to be regarded as potentially grave; no matter how benign the illness might appear to be at first, the dreaded pulmonary complications and cyanosis might set in without any notice at all. A patient might have been ill a day with mild influenza and seem to be progressing well; in an hour or two the whole picture might change, and 24 hours later the patient might be dead . . . Every case had to be regarded as in grave danger.

In Malmo, Sweden, two thousand schoolchildren were invalided. And just to confound any doctors who sought geographic or climatic links for the disease, it also attacked Johannesburg, South Africa. Among businesses and industries affected were the gold mines, where production was cut 10 per cent.

From Paris, however, came advice. "Wear a nightcap," prescribed Dr. Louis St. Maurice, a favorite with Parisian society.

His counsel had come too late for King Alfonso of Spain, who went to bed with a fever of 102.2° — undoubtedly minus a nightcap.

7

ON SUNDAY, October 6, a most unusual — and disquieting — happening aroused the six thousand residents of Clearfield, Pennsylvania, from their afternoon languor. The cry of "Extra!" rang through this coal-mining and tile-manufacturing community on the Susquehanna River, thirty-five miles north of Altoona. The streamer head gave the reason for this first Sunday edition of the morning newspaper ever to roll off the presses:

*SEVEN CASES SPANISH FLU
ARE FOUND IN CLEARFIELD*

A one-column headline in the *Clearfield Progress* below the large type explained:

NEW CHILDREN'S HOME IS
TAKEN FOR EMERGENCY
HOSPITAL BY OFFICERS

"The Spanish influenza epidemic has arrived in Clearfield," commenced the story. "Local doctors discovered seven cases of real sure enough influenza up to 3 o'clock this afternoon.

66

"As is usual with the disease, it is not located in a single section or neighborhood but is scattered throughout the town."

It had been a turbulent afternoon in the city room of the *Progress*, finding printers, pressmen and newsies. As it turned out, J. D. Connelly, the city editor, and G. A. Stewart, the managing editor, had written almost every word in the extra edition, then filled in the gaping columns with "boiler plate" — syndicate stories about potato harvesting, night life in New York City and ambulance dogs on the Italian front.

Stewart had been galvanized into action shortly after noon when John Urey, the borough solicitor, had telephoned him at home to report the results of an emergency meeting in the borough office. Two days previously, Dr. John W. Gordon, county health officer, had ordered saloons and theaters closed. As elsewhere, it had been a difficult ban to enforce. Two rural hotels, for example, ostensibly complying with the order, were allowing customers in via a circuitous route that terminated at the back door.

On Saturday, the specter of German action in hitherto peaceful, insulated Clearfield County had arisen for the first time. Sheriff Gorman at Wilson Run had arrested "a dangerous enemy alien" with the implausible name of Pusherino Blow-upsky, further described as an Austrian. Found near the mines, the stranger was said to be carrying stolen dynamite caps — and, inevitably, suspicions arose that he was also toting something even more deadly: influenza germs. All in all, it seemed none too soon to organize Clearfield.

Urey, who had distinguished himself by eliminating hogs from metropolitan Clearfield when he was first appointed borough solicitor, summoned a liberal quorum of civic leaders to his offices in the County Trust Building: Mayor Chase and Dr. William E. Reilley, president of the Board of Health, Judge Joseph E. Phillips, the Reverend Edward C. Reeve, pastor of the Presbyterian Church, and numerous ladies of the Children's Aid Society.

The presence of the latter was occasioned by the need for the new children's home. Unused, barely completed, the big yellow-brick building on Old Town Road, just beyond the Clearfield limits on the Susquehanna River, had been dubbed "the house of mystery." Two local businessmen-philanthrophists, John Rigley and Asbury Lee, had put up $18,000 each to build a home for the county's orphaned and indigent crippled children. However, possibly hoping to keep their massive gift a surprise until the day of dedication, neither Rigley nor Lee had officially announced the purpose of their huge structure. Now, as Dr. Reilley said at the meeting, the building, though unfurnished, would be ideal as an emergency influenza hospital.

In similar rapid fashion, it was voted to close down schools and churches. John Urey himself was named coordinator for all conceivable epidemic contingencies.

"It is true," Dr. Reilley conceded, "there have been no fatalities. But — we must be prepared." The ladies seconded his call, as they adopted a watchword for this new crisis, reminiscent of the rallying cry which had swept the land before America's entry into the Great War: "Preparedness!"

Borough Solicitor Urey, a pleasant man of firm purpose, had no hesitancy in employing to the fullest his new powers. If he could drive the pigs out of Clearfield, he reasoned, he could also sweep his township clean of flu germs.

First, he needed a superintendent for the new hospital. And by a stroke of the pen he at once appointed one: thirty-nine-year-old Elizabeth Clees, the county tuberculosis nurse.

Ever since she had come to the county nearly sixteen years ago, the short, slender Elizabeth had been a popular figure. The picture of her guiding her horse and buggy down Second

Street as she headed out into the county on her rounds was one familiar to every resident of Clearfield.

"There goes Nurse Clees," was a repeated observation. And each one could readily agree, "She is always doing something for somebody else." It was an obvious heritage from her late father, the Reverend Robert G. Williams, who had led a life of dedicated impoverishment amidst the squalor of Pennsylvania's coal towns. She had surprised most of Clearfield in 1917 by marrying Robbins Kimber Clees, a short, bespectacled jack-of-all-trades: watch repairer, chauffeur, mechanic, salesman for the Franklin automobile. As the Reverend Mr. Reeve, for whom Elizabeth was occasionally church organist, used to observe, "She's determined and set and can certainly order people around like no one's business." "Kim" Clees — easygoing, good-natured, but not brother to the world of business acumen — seemed to share nothing in common with his firm-jawed, steely-blue-eyed wife. Yet, though Elizabeth was a natural choice to direct the hospital, Urey had instantly thought of her this afternoon only because Kim, earlier in the day, had shambled into the borough solicitor's office to pick up a malfunctioning clock.

Soon the meeting disbanded. Urey turned his office over to two schoolteachers, Alice Lemon and his sister, Mary H. Urey. And since, in a formal kind of way, the widower Urey was courting Ella H. Fulton, a stenographer in the adjoining office, he went to the door and politely bade her "Good afternoon." To the younger Ella, John Urey remained "Mr. John." That she might indulge in the informality of "John" was to her improbable.

Now Urey hastened down the one flight of stairs in the County Trust Building, accompanied by Dr. Reilley. Together they started off in the physician's Model T for Clearfield Hospital, where Nurse Clees was working this afternoon. Soon

Elizabeth Clees was informed of her delegated grave responsibility. While "voluntary," the position was nonetheless not one the little nurse could very well refuse. She had but to think back on her father's long-ago parishes, the wretched hovels, drenched in coal smoke and coal dust, named Cochranton and Nelson, Fruit Hill, Kylertown and Snow Shoe; the dirty, hungry people whom the Reverend Mr. Williams unhesitatingly called "mine."

In the chill of Sunday evening, John Urey and Dr. Reilley drove Elizabeth back through Clearfield to her house on Ogden Street, near the river. She paused only to gather articles of clothing, and then the three continued the few blocks farther along the Susquehanna to the Children's Home, where the lights winked with unfamiliar warmth out of the dusk. Women from the Children's Aid Society had preceded the trio there. Already iron cots were being carried through the front door, bedding, chairs, and even several cases of what appeared to be groceries. The home was almost ready to swing into operation as a hospital. John Urey helped its first superintendent out of the Model T, which Dr. Reilley had parked under the portico.

"Well, Elizabeth," he said. "This is it."

Slowly, almost apprehensively, the three joined those who were filing into the home. It smelled of paint and plaster, of varnish on the stairway banisters. John Urey, hat in hand as he stepped gingerly upon the gleaming floors, was intrigued by a thought which had occurred to him on the drive over. John Rigley and Asbury Lee, who had built the place, would surely be surprised upon their next visit here. No one had asked *their* permission.

Inwardly, Urey confessed that this was the day's sole nuance of humor. It seemed to him the action was dramatically highhanded. The more he pondered this aspect the more amusing it seemed to him. But at least Clearfield, as the resolution read, was "prepared."

Otherwise there was little to smile about in the nation this gray Sunday. In many towns and cities the Sabbath was churchless, also autoless, and most certainly — spitless. In New York, police arrested five hundred persons unsuccessful in their furtive attempts at public expectoration. Fines ranged up to $25.

In Philadelphia, the epidemic was proceeding with the force and inertia of a steam roller. Dr. Cairns, president of the Board of Health, announced that 289 men and women had died of flu and pneumonia in the past twenty-four hours. The number accounted for 77 per cent of the day's total deaths, the highest rate Philadelphia had ever recorded. All Sunday patrol wagons, bells clanging, had been arriving, three and even five at a time, at the Philadelphia Hospital, where four patients expired every hour. Mrs. J. Willis Martin, president of the city's Emergency Aid, called for volunteers. Twelve physicians, appearing as if out of nowhere, were directed by police to an especially infested neighborhood. By nightfall, they had visited a thousand patients.

Residents called "Filbert 100" in such increasing volume that the telephone company doubled, then quadrupled its lines serving this number. As a matter of fact, 850 "hello girls" were themselves voiceless and sick at home. By nightfall, 5561 additional cases were burning away all Philadelphia's vigor, even the police were falling as they walked their beats. Neighboring Camden, just across the Delaware River, was also seriously affected — and Chester, a few miles south.

Dr. Wilmer Krusen, Philadelphia's health director, concerned that the citizenry should make a bad situation worse, warned against "fright or panic."

In Newport, Rhode Island, a thousand feverish sailors from

the Training Station were moved to unfamiliar territory: the Vanderbilt farm. On its neatly manicured lawns and meadows, pyramidal tents were erected, wooden walks pegged into the earth, and hoselines connected to temporary outlets. The cows and horses of this society showplace were locked in the barn, as the emergency hospital swung into operation. Ambulances chugged in and out of the high stone gates, moving a continuing two-way flow of patients and personnel.

Providence had been hit with more than five thousand cases during the past two days. Schools were closed, public gatherings banned, and churches severely regulated. Victim of the latter order was Billy Sunday, who had built a temporary tabernacle in Providence over the objections of war allocation officials. Nonetheless, the evangelist had proceeded with construction, using "surplus" lumber.

"We can meet here tonight," declared the one-time White Sox ballplayer, "and pray down an epidemic just as well as we can pray down a German victory. The whole thing is a part of their propaganda; it started over there in Spain, where they scattered germs around . . . there's nothing short of hell they haven't stooped to do since the war began. Darn their hides!" Even as he alternated prayer with damnation in this possibly last revival, members of the audience sickened and were carried from the tabernacle.

Yet if he inwardly acknowledged a foe too formidable even for him, Sunday gave not a hint. As his choirmaster and trombonist Homer Rodeheaver led a final chorus of "Brighten the Corner," 657 converts "hit the trail." He shook their hands and presented them with cards testifying to their new-found faith.

Whether Billy Sunday could "pray down" the epidemic and continue his remaining four weeks in Providence became a subject of debate. Jubilation of Rhode Island saloonkeepers, however, over the knowledge that Sunday's oratory would at least be curtailed was short-lived. Their establishments, which had been a prime target for his vituperation, were closed anyhow by the epidemic. The flu was flailing not only into the large centers of population such as Providence, but the small towns and even those which could scarcely boast the modest honor of "whistle stop." Edith L. Price, a public health nurse of Canaan, Connecticut, reported on one spot in a raging statewide epidemic:

> Working every minute from 7:45 A.M. to 6 P.M. my night work began about 8 or soon after and I would come home after 12, 3, 4, or 5:30 in the morning, sleep until 7, rise and begin over.
>
> I often used to feel like a machine going about until I ran down. The most of the cases were among Italians. . . .
>
> As it was almost impossible to get any help, I had to do a good deal myself, especially at first, of building fires, heating water and nourishment, etc. In one family, I had the parents and seven children, all bed patients. I had three full-size beds, two cots, one crib and one cradle. They lived in a four-room shanty.
>
> I usually spent two hours, sometimes longer, caring for them; the children were from one year up to 8 years. The mother was very ill with pneumonia and pregnant, father also ill with pneumonia. There was an old deaf man there who gave medicine and nourishment when I was not there.

Now Berlin, New Hampshire, was effectively destroyed as far as any activity was concerned. So in need of doctors and nurses was this community that Miss Wild, of the Metropolitan Life Insurance Company's welfare division, was sent in from her New York headquarters.

> It is hardly possible for me to describe the conditions in this community [she reported to New York]. I am the only experienced public health worker here with the exception of the staff. Saturday, with the aid of a lay worker, I cared for 40 patients, from four to nine sick in one family. Each nurse

73

is provided with a lay worker, automobile and chauffeur. Everything possible is being done. There are only seven doctors in the city. Doctors from near-about towns come in for a few hours each day. Surrounding towns are all afflicted, but not to such an extent as Berlin. There is only one 50-bed hospital in the city in charge of Catholic sisters, who have given up their own rooms as a temporary pneumonia ward. The sisters are sleeping in the school house; schools, churches and movies, etc., are closed, indefinitely.

Since starting this letter I have had to stop and do some emergency work. It was about 9 o'clock and the call was some two miles distant. I was alone at headquarters but there was a friendly-looking Ford at my disposal and we made the trip in safety, after many stops to inquire the way, and added one to the male population of Berlin. Impossible to locate a doctor.

If it seemed strange that Berlin, New Hampshire, in its mountain sanctuary, should have been singled out by the flu, it was all the more baffling to medical science that pinpricks such as Silverton, Colorado, and Belen, New Mexico, should have become targets for heavy infestation. More than half the population of both towns was ill.

Miss Mary Banzhof, the only nurse available in Silverton, reported: "Our flu scare did not stop with the flu itself. Nearly all the cases were double pneumonia and for 10 days I had to go alone with an undergraduate for help. We had 12 cases in the house and with all that had a big accident in the mine."

When night cloaked the houses of Silverton, or those of Berlin, New Hampshire, or of Clearfield or Philadelphia, there was not necessarily surcease from care or worry. Rather, with darkness apprehension was magnified. "If I should die before I wake" had become more than a phrase out of nursery-taught prayers.

8

OCTOBER was barely in its second week when Dr. H. S. Mustard, a Public Health Service epidemiologist who had been appointed "health czar" for Washington, stormed into the office of Louis Brownlow.

"If we don't keep Washington going now," asserted the specialist in malaria control to the District Commissioner, "there won't be any France!"

The evidence was plain enough for anyone to understand. There were ten thousand or more ill in the nation's capital. Brownlow had just heard from the fire marshal, for example, that so many firemen were sick "the whole city'd burn to the ground if it ever got started." The federal government was limping with one or more key workers missing from almost every office of every department. The employees at the State, War and Navy building several times daily were marched, like docile animals, out of their Victorian structure and aired for twenty minutes. Then they were shooed back to their desks in this elemental attempt to foil infection. The Senate and House of Representatives closed all galleries except those reserved for the press. District of Columbia courts recessed indefinitely.

But these measures weren't "enough," said Dr. Mustard. And he wasn't sure that face masks — "maybe as effective as fish nets against flies" — were "enough," even though every third person in Washington now wore one. Commissioner Brownlow and Dr. Mustard knew they must do something. And they *did* something.

First, they declared the entire District of Columbia a "sanitary zone." Patterned after similar emergency structures at Army camps, the zone would, in turn, be subdivided into four districts, each self-contained as to medical, nursing and volunteer staffs.

The two men also prepared a new code. One clause, for example, decreed, "No person shall knowingly expose himself or any other persons, or if he has the power and authority to prevent, permit any other person to be exposed to infection of epidemic influenza."

In other words, it was now almost against the law to get sick.

It was also "unlawful . . . for a patient to appear in public." Fines for infractions of this provision ranged from fifty dollars upward.

The pair was informed by Dr. Fowler, the health commissioner, that every hospital bed in the city was filled. In George Washington University Hospital not a single nurse was presently on duty. All of them were sick. At Garfield Hospital, cots and mattresses were stretched in the corridors. And even these had become a priority matter. Dr. Leake's emergency hospital was jammed. He was calling for anyone — even out-of-work actresses such as Flo-Flo and her "Perfect 36" chorus — to come and help him.

"The only way we could find room for the sick," he confessed, "was to have undertakers waiting at the door, ready to remove bodies as fast as the victims died. The living came in one door and the dead went out the other." The specter of the unburied dead having haunted Brownlow, he arranged with Camp Humphreys to send a contingent of fifty soldiers to dig graves — as many graves as they could dig, graves for which there were not even, as yet, bodies.

Coffins, cleanliness and nourishment dominated the thoughts of the Commissioner and the "health czar." Surprisingly enough, the two found partial answers to all three essentials that afternoon in the Potomac freight yards, south of the city. Acting on a tip from a railroad dispatcher friend, Brownlow discovered two carloads of coffins in the yards, consigned to Pittsburgh. Without concerning himself with the intricate legal aspects, he commandeered the entire shipment in the name of the District of Columbia. Thus, he reasoned, he could scotch a growing, ghoulish profiteering in such unhappy but essential merchandise. He ordered that they be stacked on the playground of Central High School, covered with tarpaulins and placed under heavy police guard. Brownlow had no illusions that even coffins were not highly desirable objects of theft.

At the same time, on an adjoining siding he espied a complete hotel kitchen and laundry plant. Both were unloaded at the Commissioner's order and placed on trucks.

Mrs. Fairchild's Red Cross motor corps, meanwhile, had been driving almost continually for the past forty-eight hours as calls rang in with ever-multiplying insistence. The women were joined by volunteers from the Central Union Mission and other charity organizations who prowled the city in search of the sick and the dead. The corps already was equipped with much codified material, including "very urgent" and "urgent" tags which were to be affixed to patients. Noon reports must be made on new cases. The District Commissioners would fine a doctor or anyone else $50 if he or she were tardy.

Esther Jonas, a young teacher at the Wilson Normal School,

had organized a kitchen in the otherwise unoccupied class-rooms. She was serving 350 meals daily to doctors, nurses, drivers and other volunteers from her zone of the city. With dual emotion, admiration and disgust, she was aware at once of "great courage" and cowardice.

"So many landlords, and landladies too," she declared, "abandoned their tenants, leaving them ill and in atrocious condition. The volunteers, however, were wonderful. They came to my kitchen in great numbers. One old lady said she couldn't do anything except wash dishes. And wash dishes she did, mountains of dishes."

In some quarters, however, Commissioner Brownlow's orders did not meet with favor. The closing of the churches, for example, had evoked cries of outrage. "It is necessary that the spiritual dynamo be kept running at full speed," admonished Dr. Wallace Radcliffe of the New York Avenue Presbyterian Church, where Lincoln once worshiped. The District Pastors Federation also condemned the ruling, suggesting that the government offices should lock their own doors. "With the theaters and movies closed," counseled a placard in the window of a piano store, "music in your home is more essential than ever." Many acknowledged the sign's truth. Once again gramophones became objects of attention. In Washington's parlors, Madame Schumann-Heink's "When the Boys Come Home" alternated with the equally popular "My Castles in the Air Are Tumbling Down," as a sort of desperate entertainment.

Among the latest victims of the flu was Mrs. Felix C. Davila, wife of the resident commissioner for Puerto Rico, and W. E. Turton, a clerk in the District of Columbia vital statistics bureau. Ironically enough, he had seemingly worn himself out in trying to keep the morbid statistics up to date. At Quantico, Virginia, Brigadier General Charles A. Doyen, who had commanded the 4th Marine Brigade at Château-Thierry, became the highest ranking officer in the armed forces to die. Recently named commandant of the Marine base, the husky, vigorous officer's sudden passing shocked his contemporaries beyond expression.

At Camp Lee, the surgeon's office reported the wave of sickness had rolled past, while at the same time expressing frustration over cause or cure:

> It is very doubtful whether any measures taken reduced the incidence of the disease. The quarantine seemed to have no ultimate effect, but did delay the appearance of the disease in the organizations so isolated. For instance, the veterinary training school of about 3800 men established a most rigorous quarantine and all members of the command had their noses and throats sprayed daily with argyrol. Consequently they had very few cases, until October 5, when the epidemic reached a sudden peak and then rapidly declined, they being practically free from disease in one week thereafter. Therefore, it would seem that the only benefit from the measures taken was that this camp was not overwhelmed at any one time by the number of sick.

While the incidence was dramatically decreasing at Camps Meade and Devens, Acting Surgeon General Vaughan nonetheless reported that five thousand soldiers had already died in training camps. His office echoed Camp Lee's despair over isolating or combating the bacteria.

Farther north, Health Director Krusen of Philadelphia announced that rainy, cool weather was driving "the influenza germs" out of the city. The Philadelphia *North American* headlined the news: THE WORST IS PAST. Dr. Krusen, certain the epidemic had "passed its zenith," predicted it would disappear "in a few days." He was insistent, however, that citizens wear their masks. In response, the Red Cross distributed fifty thousand more of the gauze objects.

In Camden, short of masks, city fathers were anxious to do *something*. "There's too much booze flowing," they finally decreed, and thereupon shut down all saloons. On Hog Island, however, in the Delaware River, 50 per cent of the workers were absent from the mushrooming shipyard complex, one of the largest in the nation. The night before, Harold W. Moffat, superintendent of hull construction, had died at Philadelphia's Misericordia Hospital.

At Harrisburg, state officials revealed that a quarter of a million Pennsylvanians were stricken.

The unseen germs, like vultures, now descended on the Jersey flatlands with the presumed object of devouring an especially pathetic horde: some ten thousand refugees from Morgan, New Jersey, where a shell plant explosion had leveled that war-born town and ten surrounding communities. Tents, cots and soup kitchens were not enough to keep out either the cold, the wet or the influenza. At Perth Amboy, five churches, a golf club and a dozen stores were converted to makeshift hospitals.

> I had whole families down with it at once [reported Miss Potts, a public health nurse in Monmouth County]. The father and eight children in one home and then the mother came down with it, and labor came on ahead of time. The man got up and almost staggered around the house, just keeping up the fire and giving milk and medicine.
>
> One forlorn little tot of three years was around and she stood by the bed patting her mother's hand, clad in a big sister's sweater that touched the ground. It was one of the careless homes, chairs without seats, panes of glass out of the windows, and doors you could not shut.
>
> None of the neighbors would come near — everyone was afraid. I almost begged one of them to do some washing, and she did it once or twice and that was all. The second day the woman's temperature was 105° and I thought we should surely lose her, but she pulled through and so did all the rest

of the family. . . . One woman nursed her husband and three boys and then came down herself. She was a heavy woman, weighing 195 pounds.

All she begged was to be left alone, she was "so tired."

The man got up and tried to do his best. I stayed there all night and in the morning telephoned to the woman's sister and she came and tapped on the window. No one would come in, but I went to the door and pulled her in and told her she had to stay. When she heard that her sister's recovery was very doubtful she was ashamed — she telephoned to another woman relative and they both helped the man out.

I went back at seven for it was a critical case, and stayed till midnight when all one could do was send for the priest.

Life was disrupted in other portions of New Jersey. At Woodbury, five weddings were halted by order of the Board of Health, fearing that the flu would be spread by such gatherings. The Rev. J. R. Larcombe, of the town's First Baptist Church, proved in a bedside ceremony, however, that influenza must not necessarily prevail over holy matrimony. He journeyed to the home of Miss Elizabeth Cooper and there married her to Lewis J. Waldbauer, of St. Louis. The nuptials, originally set for the Little Church Around the Corner in New York, had been postponed since bride and groom were ill. They still were.

With 2073 cases in the past twenty-four hours, the epidemic was increasing in New York City. "Open-faced sneezers," now America's greatest single class of public enemies, were liable to fines and jail sentences. Penalties of $250 or more were authorized against doctors who did not report new cases, as well as against landlords who were wanting with heat. A strict 4 P.M. closing hour was set for all stores. Saloons, billiard rooms and soda fountains were padlocked.

Lillian Wald, besieged with telephone calls at her Henry Street Settlement, wrote Miss Louise Mayer, of the Junior

League, for assistance. At Presbyterian Hospital, the nurses had abandoned all routine.

Until the epidemic [wrote Dorothy Deming, a student nurse], death had seemed kindly, coming to the very old, the incurably suffering or striking suddenly without the knowledge of its victims. Now, we saw death clutch cruelly and ruthlessly at vigorous, well-muscled young women in the prime of life. Flu dulled their resistance, choked their lungs, swamped their hearts . . . there was nothing but sadness and horror to this senseless waste of human life. . . .

I never saw a patient walk into the ward or come in a wheel chair; victims came on stretchers, often propped up for breathing ease.

There were no more formal "doctors' rounds," neither for the attending physicians nor for the medical students. Doctors came and went at all hours, calling for a nurse only when giving an order or needing help. It was quite usual to see a haggard doctor come in long after midnight to make a last examination of his patient before staggering home to bed. Sometimes as many as three physicians were in the ward at once, and this was true of the chaplains, priests and rabbis also. . . .

Many a morning, after working hard over a patient, Dorothy [another nurse by the same name] and I bore the grim task of trying to find words of comfort for dazed parents, husbands and children. One dawn — a glorious morning with rose-colored clouds above the gray buildings across the street — after a particularly sad death I knew the tears I had been shedding inwardly must find outlet. I rushed to the linen closet, always our place of refuge, and there ahead of me was Dorothy, sobbing her heart out. . . .

9

SPANISH INFLUENZA still eluded the best medical research. Opinions, nonetheless, continued to pyramid.

The epidemic [Dr. John Eyre, a British medical professor declared] is one of true influenza, due to *bacillus influenzae,* complicated in a large percentage of cases by secondary infections with pneumococcus or streptococcus longus . . . one or other of these secondary infections being responsible for the terminal fatal septicaemia . . .

I fail to understand the attitude of those who, confronted with the available data, refuse to accept the obvious and seek some mysterious and elusive pathological virus, filter-passer, or what not, to explain a pandemic which is the exact counterpart of the one which a quarter of a century ago prompted the investigation which led to the discovery of *bacillus influenzae.*

Dr. Albert J. Croft of Chicago voiced his theory:

I have arrived at the conclusion that if our scientists were to make a careful chemical, geological and meteorological survey of the countries now affected by the so-called influenza some irritated condition of the atmosphere would be found which would account for the cause and rapid extension of this ailment.

83

The numerous gases used on the battlefields of Europe, with their highly poisonous properties, the liberation of a large quantity of ground air high in carbon dioxide content due to trench systems, the gases from decomposing bodies and lower animals, and those set free by the destruction of cities and ammunition dumps during the last few years, may have combined to form a gaseous compound with highly toxic properties probably due to the rearrangement of molecules by the tremendous concussion produced by high explosives.

With this idea in mind I am going to advance the theory that the condition termed influenza is in reality a non-bacterial, non-contagious disease caused by the inhalation of small amounts of a depressing, highly irritating, high density gas, present in the atmosphere, especially at night and when the air is surcharged with moisture, more particularly near the surface of the earth.

Others agreed with Dr. Mustard of Washington on the subject of masks — "an absurdity, a menace when worn by the civilian population, military or naval class," according to Dr. John F. Kyle, of California. "Masks are for doctors and nurses in an operating room," he added. "They look good to the poor innocent patient and the nurses . . . Influenza is a self-limited disease and it gets you going or coming regardless of vaccines or mask."

Vaccines themselves continued to be the subject of speculation. A committee of pathologists appointed by the Massachusetts State Board of Health reported that "the evidence at hand convinces the board that the vaccines we have considered have no specific value in the treatment of influenza." Dr. Leake, in Washington, agreed, branding vaccines as "no good." His own primary object was to make patients comfortable and combat as best he could the "profound depression" which invariably took possession of all bodily workings and reactions. He kept his wards warm and the sick people well blanketed.

Even according to this philosophy, there were widely differing methods of treatment. "Give them plenty of fresh air" was the prescription of many doctors. Even in northern Minnesota and Michigan, where traces of snow had already fallen, patients were wheeled out onto porches and left there, night and day. "They need oxygen" was the reasoning behind this visibly radical therapy. "Only way to heal the lungs and prevent pneumonia."

Pneumonia was unquestionably the continuing nightmare for those who attempted to treat influenza. Even after autopsy, there was grave difference of opinion on whether the flu itself or its colleague pneumonia had brought about death. Both diseases inflamed and irritated the lung cavities until they filled with fluid, suffocating the patient and causing his entire body to become cyanotic — blue-black.

> In our patients we not infrequently found the physical signs of a patch of pneumonic consolidation in the absence of high fever, pain in the side, dyspnea, cyanosis or blood tinged with abundant sputum [reported Dr. Henry A. Christian, chief physician at the Peter Bent Brigham Hospital, Boston]. In many such patients no suspicion of pneumonia would have been aroused by ordinary observation of the case without careful and repeated examination of the lungs . . .
>
> What seems to me important is that often an influenza patient would have a drop in temperature and feel greatly relieved of his discomfort; in fact might feel well enough to get up and go out. Then his temperature would rise again and pneumonia signs would appear.

Vaguely suggestive of measles, there was frequently an attendant condition, "hyperaesthesia of the skin." This was noted especially by Navy surgeons, who described the oddity in more detail: "General flushing, sometimes papular or pustular eruption . . . sometimes skin unusually dry, sometimes sweating. Glandular swelling about the neck occasionally." These signs, like lung fluid, might be manifestations of the body's counter-blows in the life-and-death struggle with its wraithlike assailant.

In New York Dr. Martha Wollstein labored unremittingly, as though the Spanish influenza had flung down the challenge before her very feet. Even as Joseph Conrad had described a typhoon as possessing a seeming personal, directed malevolence, Martha Wollstein was convinced that the deadly bacillus — or was it a virus? — was imbued with an almost conscious purpose.

"In allen Fällen von Influenza fand sich in dem charakterischen eiterigen Bronchialsecret eine besimmte Bacillenart. . . ." The words of Richard Pfeiffer drummed through her mind like a refrain as she hurried from her apartment at 1 West 81st Street to Rockefeller Institute. Of course, she thought, there were a "variety" of bacillae in all cases of influenza. But what — what in heaven's name — was *the* bacillus?

The preceding evening, before finally switching off the lights and leaving her laboratory, she had written: "The cultivation of the Pfeiffer bacillus in interepidemic periods, from the upper respiratory tract, is not significant necessarily of clinical influenza. . . ."

Not "significant." No, she reflected, it was not. Nothing was "significant." In one frustrating emotion, she was both discouraged and fascinated by her probings. Her love of music, art, the theater had been shelved the past two weeks as she devoted her waking hours to the study of this pandemic.

With only a cup of coffee and a piece of dry toast for breakfast, Martha Wollstein was soon before her laboratory table, and at an hour well in advance of New York's normal workaday reveille. Awaiting her were the heavy artillery of the researcher: test tubes, microscope, smear slides, culture cabinets, index cards. In a few moments, now in her white apron, she began to make notes:

"It has been shown that the sera of patients convalescent from influenza yield reactions for agglutinins, precipitins, and complement-binding bodies with antigens of Pfeiffer's bacillus. . . ." Yes, it had been "shown." But what additional interpretation would her superior, the brilliant Dr. Simon Flexner, possibly place upon this, or her colleagues Dr. Peter Olitsky and Dr. J. E. McCartney?

The efforts of Dr. Wollstein and others already seemed too late. New York City, encompassing all its sprawling boroughs, from Staten Island northward to the Bronx and east to Queens, was registering 3077 new cases and more than 10 per cent mortality in the past twenty-four hours. On the lower East Side, Lillian Wald was listening to what had almost overnight become a typical report from one of her workers:

> . . . . she found the entire place in great excitement. Several pneumonia and many influenza patients were in the house and in one family three were in bed and the corpse of another had not been removed for four days. The undertaker, having more profitable clients, had not attended to their call.

There remained nothing to do but notify the department of health, already overburdened with demands.

Miss Wald was informed that the laundresses at Bellevue Hospital had panicked and "abandoned" their tubs. Resourceful as always, the Henry Street Settlement director had restaffed the laundry with domestic science instructors and students from Teachers College, Columbia University. At the same time two banker friends, who had volunteered their services "if needed," were badly needed. She started them on their way to the odorous wards and cells of Welfare Island.

By four o'clock that afternoon she was presiding over an emergency session called by the Atlantic Division of the Red Cross. The objective was to mobilize all nursing help in the city. The meeting opened on a shocking note, as Miss Schatz, of the Settlement's Visiting Nurse Service, made her report: of the 170 nurses who composed the day staff, thirty-one had already succumbed. A student nurse, Jennie Kyle Vivian, and a house physician, Dr. John Richard Perkins, died at Presbyterian Hospital. Trying to keep up with the need for more beds, the New York diet kitchen was converted to a hospital.

New York State was also crippled. All schools, churches, theaters and nonessential businesses such as poolrooms and saloons were closed in Rochester and Buffalo. Dr. Franklin C. Gram, acting health commissioner of Buffalo, announced that the city would make its own coffins and ordered Dr. F. B. Smering, chief of the bureau of sanitation and a one-time carpenter, to take charge of this unusual municipal manufacture.

"They will not be $1000 caskets, or even $100 caskets," declared an angry Dr. Gram. "They will be plain, with plain handles, and respectable . . . the casket business is a worse trust than oil. The health department will make them and will sell them at cost to the families needing them and will give them to the families of the poor."

In Rochester, averages caught up with Mrs. Susan Davis, eighty-year-old daughter of a sea captain. She had survived an infancy on sailing ships as well as a drinking husband whose fighting career did not end with the Civil War. She also had come within minutes of being aboard the ill-fated steamer *Portland* when it sailed to its wintry doom from Boston in 1898. At the home of her granddaughter, where she had long ago sought refuge from her husband, Mrs. Davis succumbed to the flu.

There was no area in the entire United States as cruelly

hurt as Philadelphia. On October 10, 528 perished from the epidemic. Nor could anyone satisfactorily explain the raging velocity of the disease in this generally neat and sober metropolis. The fire department commenced a day-long routine of hosing down streets and sidewalks, and few citizens ventured outside without gauze masks. And still the people fell. The dead lay sometimes for more than a day beside the gutters, and yet longer in half-abandoned, chill rooming houses. A mixed fear and revulsion had frustrated calls for stretcher-bearers and gravediggers.

Something had to be done, and quickly. The Rev. Dr. Joseph Corrigan, director of Catholic charities in Philadelphia, took the lead. He organized a convoy of six horse-drawn wagons and one truck. They started a twenty-four-hour continuing search for the abandoned dead. Volunteers from the diocese, including theological seminarians, accompanied him, carrying spades, shovels and kerosene lanterns. Two more doctors arrived at the Philopatrian Club, swelling its medical and volunteer staff to nearly forty men and women. The converted literary society now ranked with the larger hospitals of the state.

Baltimore was aflame with the fever. The Bureau of Communicable Diseases reported that the important Maryland port, which had been miraculously free of influenza, had somehow cultivated more than twenty thousand cases — almost overnight. Dr. John F. Hogan, assistant commissioner of health, and an expert on communicable diseases, was swamped with work. He must not only attempt to find the lair and the secret paths of the infection's transmission, but also treat cases. There were so few physicians.

He encountered challenges which had not been approximated in his fifteen years of practice. About to enter an apartment off Clifton Park, one evening, he was almost knocked off his feet by a stampede of wild-eyed women. "Doctor!" they shrieked. "Doctor! Do something, give us something!" They tore at the lapels of his coat and tugged at his sleeves. A physician was a magic, almost primitive symbol of health — and aseptic protection. In the recesses of these women's brains the instincts of witchery — and fear of that which could not be seen or even perceived — had been awakened.

Dr. Hogan realized this. He also was afraid. Tucking his bag under his arm, he lowered his head and plunged through the gathering mob of hysterical females. He streaked across the park, as though he were pursued by devils . . .

Cardinal Gibbons himself was deeply concerned over the spread of the disease. In fact, he postponed the golden jubilee of his episcopate, due to be celebrated October 20, explaining that "the joyful character of such an occasion would hardly harmonize with the suffering and sorrow that so generally prevails."

Forty miles to the south, Commissioner Brownlow received a telephone call from a woman who sounded as distraught as those who had beleaguered Dr. Hogan. The caller, explaining between sobs that she shared a room with three other girls, said that two were dead, one was dying, and that she alone was well. Brownlow, now nursing his ill wife and half sick himself, called the police. He asked them to hurry to the address given.

In a few hours a police sergeant telephoned back to the District Commissioner. "Four girls dead," was his laconic report.

Seventy per cent of Navy personnel in Washington were now afflicted, in various degrees, with the flu. The *Evening Star* of Washington inaugurated a column under the heading "Prominent People Who Have Died of Influenza." The name of Mrs. Wellington Koo, wife of the Chinese ambassador, soon appeared in this space. Though in normal times paid obituaries in the same paper filled a column, or at most two, they now swelled to half a page.

In Luray, Virginia, Mr. and Mrs. J. E. Henderson were buried in the same grave. The eighty-six-year-old Confederate veteran, who had fought with Stonewall Jackson, had never known a sick day until seized with the flu. The couple died within hours of one another.

Dominating all was a conviction of helplessness, one shared by doctor and nonprofessional alike. This attitude was given eloquent voice by the New York State Public Health Commissioner, Dr. Hermann Biggs, as he noted that the epidemic "has brought to this country a disaster of great magnitude." He could but bemoan "the almost hopeless, helpless attitude of the authorities."

Nonetheless, the struggle for life continued. There were two principal categories of people: those afflicted with the disease and those who endeavored to save them.

10

. . . Though the use of suitably constructed face masks will reduce the interchange of respiratory germs through inhalation, it must be remembered that there are many other paths by which such germs are spread, either directly or indirectly. Soiled hands, common drinking cups, improperly cleaned eating and drinking utensils in restaurants, soda fountains, etc., roller towels, infected food — these are only a few of the common vehicles of germ transmission.

CHIEF OF STAFF Peyton March was among the many highly placed officers and civilians in Washington who were seriously concerned over the unslackened acceleration of the flu. Pershing continued to cable for more replacements, his armies now being engaged in the massive Meuse-Argonne offensive and subject to war's greedy hunger.

"If we are not stopped on account of influenza," General March advised the A.E.F. Commander-in-Chief, "which has passed the 200,000 mark, you will get the replacements and all shortages of divisions up to date by November 30."

The Washington correspondent for the *Baltimore Sun* was translating into a story the latest bulletin from the Army Surgeon General's Office. It made sober reading. Noting that 9549

American lives thus far had been lost overseas in battle, the report added that more than seven thousand soldiers had already succumbed to influenza. There had been 889 deaths in the past twenty-four hours, causing the Army mortality rate to soar from 4.4 to 81.9 per thousand.

> It had [wrote the correspondent] paralyzed for a time all the plans of the War Department for marshalling the additional manpower needed to make the defeat of Germany absolutely complete. All the October calls of drafted men have been suspended, except those for a few hundred registrants to engage in limited service. Unless there is a decided improvement in the virulence of the epidemic, the November calls also will be passed over. This will put the department's program back two whole months, insofar as training is concerned. . . .
> That Spanish influenza is playing havoc with the Army notwithstanding all the precautions to prevent its spread and the application of the best medical science to it, is shown very forcibly in the report made today by the Surgeon General covering the last week. This shows that 88,478 cases of the disease were reported, as against 37,845 for the preceding week.
> There were more than 8000 additional cases of pneumonia. This is an increase of 100 per cent.

Into the Public Health Service, the Red Cross, the Army and Navy and such private organizations as the Salvation Army, YMCA, BPOE, Knights of Columbus and yet others, wires continued to crackle with urgent requests: "More doctors . . . more nurses . . . more face masks . . . more medicine . . . more blankets and pneumonia jackets!"

Surgeon General Blue, like some Aesculapian conjurer, dug still more deeply into his bag of medical tricks to produce 250 additional Public Health Service doctors. They came from old men's homes, from the warmed parlors of their married children, and from institutions for the partially debilitated. The lame, the halt and, in lesser proportions, the near-blind — they nonetheless were M.D.'s, possessing, it seemed, the secrets of salvation from this peril and even, in some cases, possibly resurrection.

The corps of old folks picked up their little black bags, dusted them off and started for all parts of the nation.

Dr. Mustard called again for "helpers and more helpers" to fight the growing epidemic in the nation's capital, where two thousand additional cases had flared overnight, a 30 per cent increase in the sickness rate. He accented his plea with a quotation from Buddha: "All men served their stricken brother save those who deserved not the name of man!"

Dr. Fowler, the health director, announced a $40 a day penalty for landlords who "refused" to supply sufficient heat for ailing tenants. The objects of his wrath, however, in many instances had a valid defense. There was no coal. Anthracite production was down 1½ million tons a month, owing to the sickness of the miners.

Appealing to Red Cross volunteers to prepare twenty-five thousand more face masks, Dr. Fowler emphasized at the same time that women's veils could not be considered a "substitute." Then, as an afterthought to his published orders, advice, and simply observations, he added: "There is no cause for panic or hysteria."

Hospital facilities in Washington would have to be expanded. In fact, they *were* being expanded as carpenters began converting a temporary War Department structure near the Potomac River. From Virginia's military camps rolled a new type of convoy: trucks bearing field kitchens and tens of thousands of hot meals for the sick and needy of the city.

The well-known and the unknown died. Among the former number was George Mosshart, Washington correspondent for the *Cincinnati Enquirer*. A much more obscure victim of the flu, Alexander Reynolds, thirty-six-year-old telephone company employee, had been alone in his apartment for three days, burning with fever. In a wild delirium, he finally slashed at his throat without success, then jumped out of the window — with success.

Hagerstown, Maryland, had canceled its annual fair. Swine were sickening with what appeared to veterinarians an infection much like influenza. Some farmers thought cattle and even poultry evidenced many of the same symptoms, while distemper in dogs seemed to be identical in its outward manifestations and miseries.

One thousand new cases had flared in the Pennsylvania Dutch hamlet of York, while Philadelphia appeared destined for a fate not far short of oblivion. There the superintendent of the morgue revealed there were 61 bodies awaiting both coffins and burial. One casket manufacturer announced he could dispose of five thousand additional caskets in two hours if only he possessed them.

Father Corrigan's somber procession, meanwhile, continued poking into back streets and alleys. His assistants moved into the dark, reeking hallways of tenements and knocked on doors. When there was no response they were compelled to force their way inside, knowing too well what in all probability awaited them. Again, the experience of Philadelphia and of Father Corrigan's efforts in particular, was somehow augured in Defoe's chronicle:

> Many houses were then left desolate, all the people being carried away dead; and, especially in an alley farther on the same side beyond the Bars, going in at the sign of Moses and Aaron, there were several houses together, which, they said, had not one person left alive in them, and some that died last in several of those houses were left a little too long before they were fetched out to be buried; the reason of which was not, as some have written very untruly, that the living were

not sufficient to bury the dead, but that the mortality was so great in the yard or alley that there was nobody left to give notice to the buriers or sextons that there were any dead bodies there to be buried. . . .

The dead carts were several times, as I have heard, found standing at the churchyard gate full of dead bodies, but neither bellman or driver or any one else with it; neither in these or many other cases did they know what bodies they had in their car, for sometimes they were let down with ropes out of balconies and out of windows, and sometimes the bearers brought them out to the car, sometimes other people . . .

In Pittsburgh, Dr. Adolph Koenig, Allegheny County medical supervisor, took a second look at the charts before him and announced that the flu had increased about 100 per cent in the past two days. In attempting to establish a regular inspection of mining communities of two or three hundred people, Dr. Koenig voiced a new fear: "The greatest danger we now have is that some small settlement might be entirely wiped out if we do not give assistance. I am convinced that Pittsburgh can handle its own situation now." While most schools were open, military classes which were to have commenced at Duquesne University were indefinitely postponed. Major E. W. Day, medical commandant of the military district of Pittsburgh, announced that the Concordia Club had been donated as a convalescent hospital for the area's hundreds of sick soldiers.

In Cleveland, Ohio, six major conventions were canceled. They included bottlers, garment workers and electrical supply groups.

In Cincinnati, where forty thousand cases had been reported, twenty-one men were fined a dollar apiece for spitting on the sidewalk. It was still more economical, by police penalty, to spit in Cincinnati than in New York, or most other large cities.

At Camp Sherman, near Chillicothe, the quarantine was lifted, although a thousand remained ill. Since the epidemic had commenced its desolation at the camp, 834 soldiers had been buried. Now there was an atmosphere of renascence at Sherman. The sergeants' rasping orders resumed, in full throat. The organizing of the 95th Division started again.

The situation was the reverse, however, at Camp Taylor, Kentucky, where 446 soldiers had succumbed to the flu, or at Camp Funston, where the current death rate was eighty-one a day, and with an increase of more than a thousand cases every twenty-four hours. This approximated the incidence at Camp Dodge, currently the Army's worst infection spot. Since the quartermaster's stock of bed sheets at Camp Funston was exhausted, Colonel Jones, the base surgeon, was forced to dig into his own pockets and buy hundreds of sheets in Topeka. "I'll probably be paying for these the rest of my life," he confided to Nurse Harding.

Camp Grant, at Rockford, Illinois, was limping, with ten thousand abed. In the past twenty-four hours, 115 soldiers had died. In no single day had there been so many fatalities at an Army training establishment. For that matter, the figure approximated the highest day's average of Americans killed in battle.

In Chicago, public funerals were regulated, as they had been in other cities. Ten mourners was decreed as both a healthy and respectful maximum. The fire department was ordered, as in Philadelphia, to keep the streets hosed down. To the Reverend J. P. Brushingham, secretary of the city's Morals Commission, however, the flu proved anew that it was truly an ill wind that blew no one good. Crime, he noted, had dropped 43 per cent in October.

Although cases were increasing in Buffalo at the rate of nearly fifteen hundred a day, city authorities saw no necessity to cancel a Fourth Liberty Loan parade. John Philip Sousa's Great Lakes Naval Training Station band had arrived to lead the parade — and lead it did. Its brassy notes brought forth young and old, all who could walk, and not a few who had to be assisted in doing so.

In New York, handbills asking for volunteers were being distributed. "Dignified and discerning women," Miss Lillian Wald declared, "stood on the steps at Altman's and Tiffany's Fifth Avenue shops and accosted passers-by." As a result of these hastily printed pleas for help, "hundreds of men and women came to the office to volunteer their services." There were no qualifications except "willingness and courage." Preconceived aversions, even social stigmas were forgotten.

"A most indefatigable worker," recalled the Henry Street Settlement director, "who could always be counted on I surmised to have been a prostitute. Her able service in one of our great hospitals won praise from the authorities and gratitude from the patients."

The largest city in the United States rushed preparations as though its gates were being stormed by some familiar, visible foe. Social leaders such as Mrs. William Randolph Hearst, who had been chairman of the Mayor's Committee of Women on National Defense, joined with other prominent ladies of New York who would do a bargain store's variety of chores from baking custards to driving through Central Park as members of a special "flying squad."

New York bureaus, such as that in charge of child welfare, suspended activities. Their employees put down their pads and pencils and scurried out with unfamiliar tools into an even less familiar world. Soon they were scrubbing floors, carrying stretchers and even digging graves.

In Brockton, the flu adamantly refused to crest. Nearly thirty persons a day continued to perish from it. There was hardly a house in Brockton which had not been touched, where tears had not been shed, even though by now most inhabitants had been dazed and pummeled almost beyond the capacity for grief. Brockton placed into operation its own tent hospital this Monday, on the grounds of the principal hospital, where Greta Lindblad nursed as a student. The virus, too, had continued to make the girls and women of her profession a prime target. Georgena and Winnifred Flemming, the sisters who had come from Nova Scotia to help at the hospital, had both died, and were buried side by side in Melrose Cemetery. Six nurses had succumbed at Brockton Hospital, and yet others were seriously ill.

Most of the cases [Greta recalled] were extremely sad, and one young girl, I believe she was a teacher, came in with flu pneumonia. She had recently become engaged and when she died after a few days' illness we removed her ring and gave it back to her fiancé. One of my cases which was especially hard for me to stay unemotional about was a young girl that I had known and played with when we were children. Her married name was Mrs. Eugene Martin. She also had flu pneumonia. She was married and about seven months pregnant. The baby was born prematurely and died at birth but I did not dare tell her that it had died. She kept begging me to see her baby and all I could do was to assure her that he was fine and beautiful and she would hold him as soon as she was stronger. She had such a lovely look on her face as she talked about her son and how happy her husband would be. It was such an effort for her to talk as her lungs were filling.

When she died late that afternoon we brought her and the baby into an empty lab room, the only available place, as they had to be prepared for the undertaker. I put the baby into her arms and fixed them so that they seemed only to be sleeping. And so the husband saw them when he came.

The flu had reached a peak in Boston. It was falling off to the point where normal civic life was being resumed and the populace already was commencing to reminisce about "the awful epidemic." Everyone had some story of his or her own.

In Quincy, a six-car hospital train which had been parked on a siding near the Fore River shipyard awaited orders to the next influenza "hot spot." Government-operated, the "Maryland Train," as it was called, had been used in Massachusetts to care for sick nurses. In charge of Dr. D. Z. Dunot of Baltimore, the original intent of this hospital on rails had been for normal sicknesses and injuries in war production areas. The city, "digging out" from the waning epidemic and even talking of folding up the tent hospitals, still was encountering reminders not only of the wreckage left in its wake but of the most debased instincts in man. In Boston's North End, the body of a twenty-three-month-old baby was discovered on a back shelf of a small undertaking establishment, partially hidden under a rubber cloth and rubbish, where it had lain for five days.

The boy's father, Leo Lafieri, told police that he had not been able to raise the $82 demanded by the undertaker.

The flu felled and it incapacitated. It materially altered both present and long-range plans of a nation which short weeks previously had thought prosecuting the Great War was its major preoccupation, its supreme challenge. Draft calls had been stopped. War construction in many industries was crippled, or halted entirely. Liberty Loan drives met telling setbacks. Even political campaigns, in a Congressional election year, had been interrupted. Many candidates, for that matter, were too hoarse to speak. This was generally conceded to be a not unleavened affliction.

Perhaps the greatest phenomenon resulting from the epidemic was the flood of advice, theories and suggested cures that cascaded into the White House and all government agencies in Washington as well as to editors of newspapers. Almost every American was hopeful that somehow — with a little more thought, or research, or a little more attention to the horoscope — an answer would be forthcoming. Yet what was it?

It has occurred to me [the Surgeon General was informed by J. Blaustein, of Springfield, Massachusetts] that possibly the epidemic of influenza may come from fish. My reason in advancing this idea is having read in the papers that submarines having been around the fishing grounds may have dropped such foods containing germs. Of course this is only a thought of mine. It might be a very foolish one.

From Boston, a man who signed himself Dr. Charles E. Page wrote to the *New York Herald* that nakedness might bring the epidemic under control:

Influenza is caused chiefly by excessive clothing on an animal by nature naked. The skin is a true breathing organ; its millions of blood vessels are forever gasping for air under even the lightest of drapery, while under the ordinary garb of many folds of clothing it is practically smothered and the blood is deprived of needed oxygen . . . We need not wonder at the high death rate.

The formula is this [wrote Mrs. Julia Gibson of Pasadena, California], saturate a piece of cotton or small clean white rag if cotton is not available, with alcohol, adding three drops of chloroform and place between the patient's teeth, letting him inhale the fumes of the alcohol and chloroform . . . it will ease the patient.

I do not happen to be very busy today [commenced Dr. A. Crichton, of Castleton, Ontario, in a letter to the War Department], so I thought it might be worthwhile to tell you that during the last few years I have written . . . explaining fully the method of treatment referred to in the printed matter I enclosed (no secret formula) and offering to go to any hospital in America at my own expense and get the results claimed, but my offer was not accepted.

His preparation, "Grippura," when used along with "other proper treatment," should cure not only the flu but lobar pneumonia, la grippe, rheumatism, typhoid fever, whooping cough and scarlet fever as well. At the same time, Secretary of the Interior Franklin K. Lane received unsigned advice from Amarillo, Texas, referring to a remedy "an old Mexican man" had given him:

> Almost a sure cure is inhaling smoke from wood or wet or damp straw or hay that will not burn very fast but make a good smoke and inhale for 10 minutes or so, and a few treatments will cure it. He says it starts in the nasal cavities and not in the throat as some think but finally reaches the throat organs. Also says that this treatment will cure the most obstinate cases of Hay Fever. Burn oak, hickory, ash wood, also corn cobs, anything that will make good smoke and it will kill the germs.

An elderly Georgia doctor forwarded information on his own cure to the *Atlanta Constitution,* recalling that in 1897 he had avoided yellow fever in Louisiana by sprinkling sulphur in his shoes:

> I believe when the system is thoroughly saturated with the sulphur, as suggested, it will prevent the germs of any disease from attacking the system. There is no doubt the sulphur will penetrate the system readily, for when one takes sulphur in the system and has a silver dollar in his pocket, it will be turned black, caused by the sulphuretted hydrogen. Try it and see. Now it would be very little trouble to have the boys in the camps carry out this suggestion and thus break up the disease which is causing so much suffering and a great many deaths.

From Chickasha, Oklahoma, Dr. Alexander B. Leeds suggested that the flu could be cured by pulling out teeth and tonsils. In Los Angeles, Dr. A. W. Cottrell said that he had isolated the influenza bacillus in 1898: "of the facultative aerobic classification . . . its habitat the blood."

Even *Popular Science*, caught up in the passions of the hour, suggested a method which would enable a cigarette smoker to enjoy tobacco while still wearing his mask. Involved were adhesive tape and a cork — the cork, to plug the hole in the adhesive, just round enough to admit a cigarette, while not actually smoking.

And somehow illustrative of the fears, the hysteria, the lunacy and the almost universal desire for escape or refuge was a ceremony in Moorestown, New Jersey. There many of the citizens turned out for the funeral of a twenty-five-year-old canary which had belonged to Harry Chambers. It had been a familiar sight caged on the porch of his East Main Street home.

As one of the mourners said in eulogy: "It used to chirp at me."

11

Necropsy 3958 — Patient entered Base Hospital 8, October 8, 1918, from a newly arrived transport. He died at 4 A.M. October 15. Pericardial cavity contains about 10 c.c. of a clear yellow fluid. There are numerous hemorrhages on the left side of the pericardium. The right lung is adherent posteriorly and the right pleural cavity contains about 300 c.c. of a cloudy yellow fluid . . .

A T ST. NAZAIRE, American and French doctors were desperately engaged with the sick. A convoy of eight transports had been unloading the past two days. En route there had been 2610 cases of flu, and 2873 during the disembarking. There had been 265 burials at sea, and now the recently arrived A.E.F. soldiers were dying in St. Nazaire at the rate of three every hour, comparable to the battle attrition on the American front.

In Chaumont, Dr. Harvey Cushing of Boston, who had established the first overseas base hospital for the Army, was feverish himself, but he continued brain surgery on the wounded. All of the A.E.F. hospitals, he reported, were "107 per cent full," influenza and pneumonia cases accounting for the surplus. Battle casualties were arriving in field and base hospitals at a "normal and anticipated rate." Nature, in the form of the epidemic, had again exceeded man in his affinity for self-destruction.

Another Bostonian, Mildred Aldrich, had been nursing the wounded at her house overlooking the Marne. Now she was faced with human wreckage from other causes. "My entire household," she wrote, "is down with the grippe. I ask myself if one reason we have so much illness is because it is so difficult for most people to keep clean. We lacked soap here for a long time. It is almost impossible to get any washing done. Luckily, I buy soap in rather large quantities." But neither Mildred Aldrich nor the nurses, nor even the doctors with whom she came into daily contact, could scrub away the flu or pneumonia germs any more than they could banish the epidemic by wishing it gone.

About 2 A.M. Lieutenant Frank A. Holden of the 328th Infantry, 82d Division, a former lawyer from Athens, Georgia, was moving through a cold rain and inky blackness somewhere near Châtel Chéhéry in the Argonne.

When we came to the crossroads [he recalled], I decided to take a nearer road to the supply company and as it happened was very unlucky in doing so because about three miles from there we met a French outfit going toward the front. Here we got into an awful jam again. I was so tired that I almost fell asleep on my horse at times when we had to stop awhile because of the roads being blocked. Only once or twice did I hear the French soldiers say anything as the rain-soaked blue columns tramped by. The newness of war with them had worn into a serious affair during the four years past.

When we arrived at the supply company we unhitched our horses and I went to the supply company tent. I found it filled with replacement officers who had just come up to fill the vacant files. I managed to squeeze in on the cold ground and slept for a few hours.

About daybreak everyone left the tent but me. I tried to get up but could not. I had such a pain in my head and chest and was suffering so that I was unable to get up with the others. My chest felt as though needles were sticking in it when I tried to cough. After breakfast several came in and felt my head and said I had a high fever. I told one of my drivers to take charge of our wagons.

About 5:00 o'clock that afternoon Charles Goodreau, from Fall River, Mass., helped me over to a nearby tent hospital.

I had to stop several times and rest before we reached the hospital. On our last stop as I sat down by the roadside I looked up and saw a German plane dive out of a clear sky towards one of our large observation balloons, and puncture it with bullets. The walls of the balloon closed in and a great cloud of black smoke gushed upward. Out from the little basket underneath jumped a small figure, the parachute opened up and the observer floated safely down from his destroyed post. The German airman, accomplishing his mission, ascended towards the left in a large semi-circle and headed back towards the German lines with the swiftness of an eagle.

The tent hospital to which I went was located on the edge of where the town of Varennes used to be. Here a doctor examined me, took my temperature which registered 103½ and tagged me acute bronchitis. I begged him not to send me back to the rear but my pleadings did no good. Then I insisted that I would not take a wounded man's place in the ambulance.

I lay down inside the tent. Ambulances and trucks would come up to get the wounded and sick but I waited for about an hour and a half before I would let them put me in a truck. Yet I wished I had been wounded because most of them were only slightly wounded and were not suffering much; they were laughing and joking. . . .

I seemed to have gotten worse. A few shells dropped near the tent and I thought we were in for a shelling but only a few hit near us.

Just outside the tent a man began singing "Mother Machree." I was already thinking of my mother before he began singing because I thought I was dying, and you know whom we want by our side when we feel that we are about to leave this world. And she no doubt was thinking and praying for me, because as Frank L. Stanton wrote:

"There's a woman a-dreaming when shadows fall drear —
Dreams of a boy Over There;
And there's light in the dream, and that Light is a prayer
Of Love for a boy Over There.
And the dream and the prayer find their way o'er the foam."

Very few ever have the experience of feeling that they are dying and live to tell it. Many are cut off from this world in a second's time and are never conscious of the fact that they are leaving.

I know now how the boys felt so far away from home who were conscious before they died and felt that they were dying.

About 8:00 o'clock that night I was put in a truck and carried to a field hospital further back of the lines. Here I took off my clothes and shoes which were still wet from the rains of the night before and I slept till morning on a cot near the stove.

"Three-day fever" was the tag put on the flu by Army doctors. The impartiality of the disease had resulted in the same number of casualties among the armies of the Kaiser. Thus it did not add up to military advantage or disadvantage for either side. Nothing, for that matter, could apparently stop the retreat of the German troops, at last set in motion.

Wild reports were filtering out of Germany. Philip Gibbs, the usually reliable English war correspondent, reported, for example, that a number of German soldiers, sick with flu, had been locked in a building at St. Amand. Then the structure was pounded to pieces by artillery as the healthy troops retreated.

In Paris, exhausted from slogging through the mud of the Argonne, Don Martin, well-known *New York Herald* correspondent, died of the flu. He had been ill less than forty-eight hours. There were five thousand cases of influenza in Barcelona and still more in Gothenburg, where Swedish doctors recorded "many" fatalities and an increasing incidence.

"It is really difficult to say," admitted the chief medical officer of London to the editor of *The Times*, "whether there has been an increase or decrease of influenza cases." The best available figures, however, showed that eighty persons had died in London, in the past seven days, compared with seventeen the preceding week. Over the lonely slopes of Tottenham Cemetery volleys had just rung out. There, in the Heroes' Corner, two nurses of Edmonton Military Hospital, flu victims, had been buried with military honors. The epidemic had also returned to Glasgow, hit four times as hard as London, to Liverpool, to Dublin, and smaller Irish communities.

Tangier, "totally unprepared," was struggling for its life. With no statistics available, the correspondent for *The Times* of London reported, "the number of deaths can only be judged by the frequent funerals met with in the streets." The roads leading out of the North African city were in such a deplorable shape that hearses mired down en route to the cemeteries.

"Unprecedented scenes" were taking place in Capetown, suffering with fourteen thousand flu ill. Farther up the east coast, eight thousand were sick in Durban. Travelers returning from the East told hardly credible tales of the Hooghly River, flowing muddily from Calcutta into the Bay of Bengal, being "choked with bodies." The Associated Press, however, made a meticulous survey of various government bureaus in this sprawling land of dust and heat and filth and came up with a story which, indeed, was almost unbelievable.

Almost 5,000,000 persons have died in British India from Spanish influenza, and fully a million others are believed to have died in the native states from the same cause, according to a report of the Indian Government made public here. The area affected contained a population of 238,026,240 and the number of deaths was 4,899,725, or 20.6 deaths per 1,000.

In a few months, it is observed, influenza claimed half as many victims as did the dreaded plague in a period of twenty years.

The influenza was particularly fatal in the central, northern and western portions, while in Burma it was not so severe. No part of Punjab escaped.

The hospitals were so choked it was impossible quickly to remove the dead to make room for the dying. Streets and lanes of the cities were littered with dead and dying people, and the postal and telegraph services were completely demoralized.

Burning ghats and burial grounds were literally piled with corpses, while an even greater number awaited removal from houses and hospitals. The depleted medical service, itself sorely stricken by the epidemic, was incapable of dealing with more than a minute fraction of the sickness requiring attention.

In the lonely islands of the South Pacific, where respiratory diseases were uncommon, if not almost unknown, natives and whites alike "died like flies," according to one correspondent. Grown men, as it turned out, were the easiest victims, while children proved almost immune. From Rewa, in the Fiji Islands, Alick Rea, a representative of the Colonial Sugar Refining Company of Sydney, wrote:

For a full week I was the only person moving about in this particular district. Not another soul was to be seen. Everything was still and quiet. Cattle were unattended and helped themselves to growing crops of rice and sugar-cane. Bananas ripened on the trees and afterward turned to vinegar on the ground. In the early hours of the evening, when the Indian coolies invariably contrive to make a blatant noise, it seemed hard to believe that one was actually on a plantation, so profound was the silence.

Soon, however, there was any amount of noise all night long — the hacking cough of the unfortunates who had developed pneumonia as a complication. Then deaths occurred so quickly that it was only with the greatest difficulty that sepulture could be given to the remains.

In the pretty little nook at Wai Ha, where Europeans are usually buried on the Rewa River, and where a funeral takes place about once in two years, there are over a dozen new mounds. These are the graves of some of our white population — heroes who gave their lives in the service of humanity as surely as any soldier had done in the war. It is to the everlasting credit of the whites that no one shirked. So serious was the position among the Indians and Fijians that the mortality would have been appalling but for the way the Europeans worked.

Practically every white man was down sick at the end of the second week's work. As there was only one doctor, all the whites had to be carried to one center, where a temporary hospital was arranged.

The epidemic, strangely enough, seemed to hit hard among carpenters, and there was only one man left who could make a coffin. As it was not certain how long this man would last, he made full use of his time getting coffins ready for what were considered the most dangerous cases. Some of these cases pulled through, and I heard one man grumbling about having to pay for a coffin that he never used. Our esteemed parson had a coffin made for himself, but he is walking about again!

More than a thousand children were orphaned in Samoa, and the native chieftains were attempting to place them under the care of the New Zealand government. Some placed the total Samoan dead already at eight thousand, two thirds of the number being men. Describing the ravages in the Samoan group, an archipelago usually ravaged by forces quite different — typhoons — the *Sydney Daily Telegraph* correspondent wrote:

As at one time 80 or 90 per cent of the people were lying helpless, many died from starvation who might probably have recovered, for even when rice, milk, and other items were sent out and delivered, the survivors were too weak to prepare and apportion the food. One day the burials in Apia numbered seventy-one, and probably out of this small town and its environs nearly seven hundred were buried.

The New Zealand troopers with their motor-trucks did wonderful service day after day gathering up the dead, who were simply lifted out of their houses as they lay on their sleeping-mats. The mats were wrapt around them, and they were deposited in one great pit at Vaimea after it was found impossible to get laborers to dig individual graves. There were no mourners, there was no ceremony. As fast as the different motor-trucks came the bodies were placed in the pit by heroic workers, who were many of them quite unfit and who had constantly to quit as they themselves became infected.

Most of the great chiefs of Samoa are buried, as well as most of the mission teachers, and 56 per cent of the government officials. Of those who passed away probably 66 per cent were adult males. A good many women also went, and some children, altho the latter were largely immune. The natives justly draw comparisons with the comfortable state of affairs at Pago Pago [the American naval station in Samoa], where sensible quarantine regulations kept the port clean.

New Zealand recorded an estimated six thousand influenza deaths. The scourge, observed Sir John Denniston, chairman of a newly organized committee to study the disease and its havoc, was "one of the gravest calamities which ever befell the people of the Dominion."

Few countries the world over — few island kingdoms, or even outposts of civilization astride the tundra or in the jungles — did not share in this tragedy. The microbes had struck dispassionately over vast terrestrial distances, without fear, or favor — or mercy.

12

"DUST MAY BE a medium in transmitting disease. Tubercle bacilli have been found in street dust. Streptococci have been recovered from floor dust."

Acting Surgeon General Victor Vaughan had made this observation, though with certain reservations. Before him was a report from Camp Funston:

> Severe windstorms seem to have a bad effect on spreading disease. At Detention Camp No. 2, the epidemic increased in intensity until the Sixth of October when 410 men were transferred to the hospital, and on the seventh of October the number was increased by 224 more. On this date, a stiff wind blew from the southwest, causing a dust storm to prevail during the entire day, on the eighth there was a marked increase in the number of cases, 675 men being sent to the hospital during the day. The increase was largely attributed to the dust storm during the day.

On the other hand, at badly infected camps such as Devens, Grant and Beauregard, the weather had been damp and cool — therefore the dust was at a minimum. Dr. Vaughan was not convinced that dust was the culprit, even though he had to admit that the dust storm at Funston before the initial outbreak in March was surely a coincidence — if coincidence it were. At this Kansas cantonment, perhaps the incubator of the world-wide epidemic, other conclusions were now being reached as October neared the midpoint:

> It was found [wrote a camp surgeon] that 17 out of 25 hospital attendants and influenza contacts contracted influenza even though a protargol spray was used vigorously. Among 25 other men who were not sprayed, but one case developed. All 50 wore masks and worked in the same temporary hospital under the same condition. It was the feeling here that wholesale spraying actually spread the infection through the common use of an atomizer.

California had been spared although the state was reacting vigorously. The armed quarantining of the Training Station on Goat Island had been an early precaution on the West Coast. Now a dread, already familiar elsewhere, attacked the movie mills of Hollywood, as the klieg lights winked out first at the Mack Sennett, then the Triangle studios. There was grave doubt whether films scheduled for other studios, starring such favorites as Norma Talmadge, Wallace Reid, Lila Lee and Charlie Chaplin, would actually be shot.

At the County Hospital in Los Angeles, the action of the nurses was something less than heroic. A total of 127 of the girls threatened to strike if the institution went through with plans to admit four Negro student nurses. At Arcadia, California, health officials rigged up a tire pump in combination with rubber tubing and gallon jugs, then commenced spraying the throats of soldiers and civilians with an "anti-pneumonia" serum. Children were frequently discovered going through the line twice and even the third time.

Duluth, Minnesota, was feeling the full aftermath of a forest fire which had leveled fourteen communities within a fifty-mile radius of the city, claimed almost a thousand lives and left a hundred thousand persons homeless. The city armory was turned over to the refugees, who spread their blankets on the bare floors. When the structure reached capacity, schools were commandeered.

> Crowded morgues in centers for refugees are ghastly meeting places for the living and the dead [wrote the correspondent for the *Minneapolis Morning Tribune*]. The destitution in and near Moose Lake, where Adjutant General Rhinow and his staff, in charge of relief work, have made their headquarters, is the most pitiable.
>
> More than 100 children, terror-stricken at the experience through which they passed, have been brought into the city from hiding places in which they crouched together, and are being cared for by the Red Cross nurses while search is made for their parents.

The coughs, the sneezes, the muscle aches inevitably began their inroads among the unfortunate people. Twenty-seven were already dead. Other sections of Minnesota were experiencing the effects of the flu, with 412 new cases in Minneapolis alone.

The smoke from the fires spread a yellow-hued veil over Midwestern skies, extending down even to Cincinnati, and adding another sensory dimension to the apprehension and unhappiness upon the land. St. Louis closed its motion picture theaters, while East St. Louis locked every public building, including churches. The Elks Lodge in Evansville was converted into one more of the nation's mushrooming flu hospitals as the disease rolled across Indiana like the mysterious blights which in some seasons struck the state's corn crop.

In Chicago, Janet Geister, a nurse with the Federal Children's Bureau, noted one "striking thing" about the epidemic. "It acted as a cyclone does; it dipped down to blast one area, only to rise and let others almost strictly alone. There seemed to be no accounting for the heavy toll it would take in one area, and its light toll in others. And in the same erratic way it would prostrate a whole family in a neighborhood that had no other cases." Janet could only conclude that "Doctors were working against a vicious foe — an unidentified one, that killed quickly and ruthlessly despite every care known to medical science . . . They didn't know what to try next."

Health Commissioner Robertson commented despairingly that the people might as well wear face masks if it did anything at all to bolster their morale. "It is our duty to keep the people from fear," he observed, in admitting medical helplessness to conquer the disease itself. "Worry kills more people than the epidemic. For my part let them wear a rabbit's foot on a watch chain if they want it."

In Atlanta, Georgia, where schools and theaters had been closed, there had been examples of greed and inhumanity. W. H. White, Jr., president of the city's Chamber of Commerce, revealed that landlords had evicted tenants simply because of their misfortune in being stricken with influenza.

"I certainly deplore the fact that such a condition should exist in Atlanta," White asserted. "Every instance of this kind works to the detriment of the city. The housing committee will certainly be glad to investigate all such complaints brought to our attention." One complaint was from an Army officer, turned out of his Peachtree Street apartment with a 103° fever. At the same time, the *Atlanta Constitution* reported, "An effort to estimate the number of cases of influenza in the city proved without result as no figures are obtainable anywhere in the city to show how many victims have been claimed here." The extent of the flu in Georgia's capital did not apparently merit the closing of schools or any public areas. Dr. J. P. Kennedy, the city health officer, said that perhaps there might be as many as eighty new cases. He conceded it to be scarcely an awesome total.

Elsewhere the epidemic continued with ever-increasing fury. In the Pittsburgh area more and more schools were closed, while tent hospitals and food centers were erected on playgrounds. In Braddock, however, it was decided to re-open the schools. As had been the experience in many sections of New York City, classrooms were often far cleaner and better ventilated than the rooms in which the children lived.

Burdened with aspirin, quinine, ointments, whiskey and rubbing alcohol, Cecil Bloom, the druggist, arrived at the Clearfield, Pennsylvania, emergency hospital. There were at least thirty cases in the borough, and the first two deaths had already been recorded. Recognizing the increasing seriousness of the Clearfield epidemic, the state health department had sent a special nurse to the town. She would bolster the efforts of such as Elizabeth Clees. Bloom, while several years Mrs. Clees's junior, had developed a fatherly concern for her well-being.

"Elizabeth," he counseled, "you have no right to take on such added responsibility, especially at your age."

"I'm only thirty-nine," she replied with a frown. "Besides, I have to. Who will take care of *them,* if I do not?"

There were still empty beds in her hospital. She was not as yet overburdened. Bloom also knew the folly of arguing with the positive, determined Elizabeth. The high school was being turned into a second hospital, although there was no certainty at the moment it would be used. Kim Clees himself had found work as an errand "boy," driver and general handyman at this latest emergency project. The prospects in Clearfield seemed altogether propitious, and the *Progress* was preparing a banner: LOCAL SITUATION FINE. With only five doctors whose full services could be counted on to treat a population of 100,000, Clearfield County nonetheless remained a bacterial powder keg.

On Sunday, the Reverend Mr. Reeve received a telegram from Camp Lee, Virginia. Edith Viberg, who sang in his choir and who had left Clearfield for new nursing duties two weeks ago, had herself succumbed to influenza. The minister, disbelieving, could still hear them singing Edith's favorite hymn at her good-by party, while Elizabeth Clees played the organ:

> I love to tell the story
>   Of unseen things above,
> Of Jesus and his glory,
>   Of Jesus and his love.
> I love to tell the story,
>   Because I know it's true:
> It satisfies my longings
>   As nothing else can do.

In Norristown, Pennsylvania, the mystery of Clarence V. Lee, a missing rural mail carrier from Marlboro, Massachusetts, was finally solved. He was found in a hotel, slowly recovering from the flu. Several days before, he had wandered off his route, feverish, not knowing where he was going, or even who he was. He had no idea how he had arrived in Norristown, but memory as well as health was returning. And that was what mattered.

In Washington, Surgeon General Blue still sought more medical personnel, though he had to admit he did not know where they would come from. Indeed, since his last over-age corps had gone forth, he held out scant hope that there were any more. "It is important," he warned as an alternative, "that people stop calling doctors and nurses unnecessarily in mild cases of influenza." The "present generation" he criticized as "spoiled by having had expert medical and nursing care readily available." Those who were not desperately ill, he advised, should go to bed "in a well-ventilated room" and "take castor oil."

Health Officer Fowler of the District of Columbia was almost as sorely tried as his friend Rupert Blue. He was particularly angered at what he denounced as "the coffin trust," responsible, it seemed to him, for gouging bereaved families on the price of funerals. He had heard of a young woman war worker from Oklahoma who had died in Washington. Two of her friends arranged to have the body prepared for shipment and then sent home. The bill soared to $350, more than the girls' combined salaries for an entire month.

"Such preying on unfortunate families," angrily declared the city's health director, "in this direful time is nothing short of ghoulish in spirit and unpatriotic to the point of treason."

In Philadelphia, Frank Paul, chief of the coroner's bureau of investigation, revealed that certain cemeteries were collecting $15 burial fees, then informing the bereaved they would have to dig the graves and bury their own. Some druggists in the same city were charging $52.40 a gallon for prescription whiskey. In New York, where 409 persons had succumbed to influenza-pneumonia in the past twenty-four hours, the situation as to profiteering was no better.

Thus had the flu brought out the best and the worst in mankind. Faced with eternity, men and women reacted along the same general patterns of conduct and morality which marked their individual behaviors in more normal times. The patterns now were simply exaggerated. The bad proved themselves pre-eminently bad. The merely foolish became chickenheaded and crazed with panic. The good, by their deeds, approximated sainthood.

Certainly America had become a praying nation, even though supplication was a fresh experience to many who indulged in it. In Providence, Billy Sunday returned to his pulpit to exult that he had fulfilled his promise to "pray down" the epidemic, which had not materialized in that city. There was talk of reopening the schools. Deriding those who depended on medicine alone, the evangelist evoked guffaws as he told of a patient who "had taken so many pills that his joints were ball-bearing"!

It was mid-evening before the revivalist finally asked choir leader Rodeheaver to terminate the session. The latter was soon goading the worshipers into a throbbing chorus of a favorite:

> Oh joy, oh delight to go without dying,
> No sickness, no sadness, no sorrow, no crying!
> Caught up with the Lord in the clouds of glory
> When He comes to receive the world His own!

Unquestionably Sunday and all of his congregation were sincere in their prayers, as sincere as were the devout of all faiths who turned to the Lord in these hours of frightened need. The vexing aspect was, however, that the microbes slew the good along with the wicked, or partly wicked. There was no recognizable distinction, no favoritism. Churchgoer and atheist were abruptly returned together to the same dust whence they had sprung.

The epidemic, like the surgings of the sea in a gale, rose and fell, with sardonic and imperturbable indifference as to whosoever might chance across its path. And none were more heartsick and frustrated than the overworked doctors themselves.

"The sudden and unexpected onset of influenza," asserted Dr. George M. Price, New York sanitation specialist, "has caught the country unawares and found the public health administration unprepared to deal properly with the spread of the disease." Dr. Vaughan himself was already numbed at beholding this pathological Armageddon, a calamity he had never anticipated in his considerable span.

"The saddest part of my life," he confessed, "was when I witnessed the hundreds of deaths of the soldiers in the Army camps and did not know what to do. At that moment I decided never again to prate about the great achievements of medical science and to humbly admit our dense ignorance in this case."

No one knew quite where to turn, but everyone was disturbed. Perhaps, speculated some, money more wisely spent in the past could have alleviated the intensity of the scourge if not prevented it altogether.

"Billions of dollars," thumped *Survey*, "have been willingly spent by the country for destructive purposes; it seems to the public health forces but rational to think that the one or several hundred million dollars which would be needed for health preparedness and fighting epidemics on a large scale would be well spent and could be well afforded by a great and rich country."

Or possibly the little things would matter, the sort of straws, however, that never in all human experience had saved one drowning man.

"Stop circulating books!" was the cry in New York City. And the public library, closing its doors, obeyed.

"Stop shaving!" was the almost hysterical order in many cities, as barbershops were padlocked, or the barbers made to swathe themselves in such ample and obstructing masks that they could not do their work in any event. In some areas the sale of safety razors soared. In others men simply let their beards grow, and the resulting byways assumed a marked Biblical flavor.

"Wear fresh pajamas!" was another tocsin. And in but one city alone the Red Cross, shoulder to shoulder with garment workers, turned out two thousand pairs in twenty-four hours.

"Abandon the universal practice of shaking hands," counseled Captain George T. Palmer of the Army Sanitary Corps. "Substitute some other less intimate method of salutation!" And a methodical *Science* reporter seconded the captain as he counted "119 chances for contact" with potential infection-spreading objects in the course of a day: from turning doorknobs to paying trolley fares.

Take castor oil! Don't take castor oil! Exercise as often as you can! Remain home and rest! Don't ride the subways! Travel under the surface if possible; there are less germs! Wear a veil! Don't wear a veil!

And so the nightmare of advice, orders and contradictions spewed forth, like the impossible conversation when Alice sat down at the mad tea party.

Where had the epidemic come from, what was it, from which of the 119 daily contacts — if any one — was it transmitted, and how, how, once contracted, could its ravages be thwarted? Obviously its leechlike grip on a victim could not be broken by wishing, or by the gyrations associated with a dog shaking off water. But how?

America's pattern of living had been utterly disrupted by these invisible assaulters, and October had not attained even a halfway point. The dread, the silence and the mortal apprehension which lay upon city and town was analogous to the pall which San Francisco had known after the earthquake, Johnstown after the flood, or Chicago after the fire. Commerce and industry of all magnitudes had been paralyzed. From factory to corner grocery store, business had slowed and slowed until it seemed to some that, given just a few more days, possibly a week or two, activity in the United States would be on a par with that of a Carthage or Pompeii long ago. The draft was at a standstill. The camps themselves were an agony of sickness.

The country was terribly mauled and still no one, no one knew what to do. It was like a hopeless, plaintive refrain: *No one knew what to do, or in what direction to turn.*

No one knew what to do.

13

Headache was a pronounced symptom in nearly all the cases, the simple influenza as well as the pneumonic. Sometimes the whole head ached and throbbed, sometimes the head did not ache if the patient kept quite still, but swam and ached all over if it was turned quickly or if the patient sat up or coughed. Besides this generalized headache, however, and often in addition to it, there was complaint of special aching, at the back of the eyes, or inside the head in front, the patient generally putting his hand low down across the forehead to indicate the site. The more generalized headache was doubtless due to the toxaemic state, thus corresponding with the aching limbs and back. . . .

CHICAGO had a dangerous, corporate headache of its own. The city, with five thousand new cases daily, was frightened. Accenting its misery, there were not enough hearses. The 159 owned by undertaking establishments added up to an insufficient half of the daily death rate. Hoping to compensate for the lack, the Cook County coroner asked the transit system to drape several trolleys in black, as makeshift hearses.

The movies were sealed. Dorothy Gish, as in Washington, would have to pause for breath once again in her *Battling*

EPORTS SHOW EPIDEMIC IS MAKING GAINS

spitals Are Filled With atients and Tents Have Been Ordered

NY SCHOOLS CLOSE

w cases of influenza reported to the d of Health during the 24 hours at 4 o'clock yesterday afternoon ate that the epidemic has taken a for the worse in Pittsburgh. For period of time 813 new cases are on d, compared with 873 for 32 hours ining Saturday noon. The total er of influenza cases was 4,445, a the new pneumonia cases number aking a total of 319. Deaths from nonia were 39, from influenza-nonia, 30, and from influenza, 5, ng a total number of 74 for the 24

AYOR ASKS OUNCIL FOR $100,000 TO HELP CHECK INFLUENZA

Deaths and 1,260 New Cases Are Reported.

SEASE MAY BE ON WANE

a emergency ordinance provid-$100,000 with which to meet the ads of influenza was introduced ouncil yesterday by Mayor E. V. cock and Controller E. S. Mor-The measure will be acted a today when, it is probable, the unt will be reduced in committ-Mayor Babcock said there was immediate change in the situa-and that the action was taken tine with the administration's to take proper preventative and active steps.

UNTY TO GIVE AID

Annex to Courthouse Is Made Emergency Influenza Hospital

Pgh. Post   October 26, 1918

Courthouse annex on Ross street will be opened this morning by the city as another emergency influenza hospital

URGENT CALLS SENT OUT BY RED CROSS

More Men and Women Needed to Aid in Com-batting Spanish Influenza.

VOLUNTEERING SLOW

CATHOLIC AID IN EPIDEMIC IS ACCEPTED

Bishop Canevin Informs Health Director of 27 New Relief Stations.

SISTERS AS NURSES

Ban Remains; Babcock Goes To Harrisburg

State Commissioner Re-fuses to Modify Health Regulations Here.

NEW CASES FEWER

Encouragement Found in Reports on Influenza and

---

converted into an experimental labora-

DRUG TRADE HAS BROKEN DOWN UNDER DEMAND FOR GRIP CURES

One Wholesale House Compelled to Close Its Doors.

KINGSLEY HOUSE GETS PATIENTS

Pittsburgh's drug trade has all but broken down under the demands

WORST IS OVER IN EPIDEMIC, AVERS HEALTH OFFICIAL

New Cases On the Wane, But Deaths to Increase, Opinion of Dr. Phillip E. Marks.

TOTAL OF PATIENTS, 14,634

The worst is over in Pittsburgh's influenza epidemic, so far as new cases are concerned, in the opinion of Dr. Phillip E. Marks, head of the bureau of infectious diseases, who stated that the situation so far this week is much better than it was at the same time last week. New cases of influenza reported today number 625, or about the same as yesterday, making total of 14,634 cases on record here.

NFLUENZA ORPHANS IN NEED OF HOMES

CITY IS ASKED BY NORTHERN COUNTIES FOR AID TO CHECK GRIP EPIDEMIC

Pgh.   Post

Pittsburgh Conditions Are Satisfactory, Of-ficials Declare.

October 13, 1918

CHURCH SERVICES BANNED TODAY

Influenza conditions in Pitts-burgh yesterday were such that medical authorities were devoting much of their energies to prepara-tion for epidemic outbreaks in other parts of Western Pennsylva-nia. Pittsburgh has been empow-ered to handle matters in this part of the state, and calls were coming in from northern counties for as-sistance.

Dr. Adolph Koenig, county med-ical supervisor, is arranging to hold

CITY HEALTH BOARD MAY GET POWER TO LIFT BAN HERE SOON

Epidemic Peak Reached Week Ago, Claim.

Influenza, as an epidemic, reached its peak in Pittsburgh on Tuesday, Wednesday and Thursday of last week, was the opinion of Dr. Wil-mer R. Batt, state registrar, after an examination of the situation yes-terday, and it is believed that his report to Harrisburg will be fol-lowed by a decision to allow Pitts-burgh authorities to dispose of the ban here at their pleasure.

Sample of Pittsburgh Headlines — Typical Rapid Surge and Ebb of Influenza Epidemic

Brigadier General Charles Doyen,
Marine Hero and Highest
Ranking Officer to Succumb

Soldiers of the A.E.F. Debarking Sick and Half Sick

Influenza Virus (Isolated 1933) Photographed by Electron Microscope. Twenty Million Fit a Pinhead.

Elizabeth Clees,
Courageous and
Heroic Nurse

Doughboys Do Wash on Orne Bank — No Help to Flu

Typical Emergency Hospital — Corey Hill, Brookline, Massachusetts

Water Supply, Tent Hospital

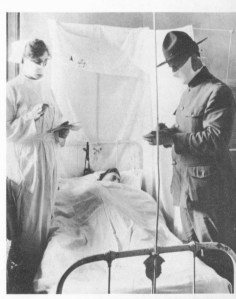

Alternating Heads of Beds and Masks, Supposed Preventives

A Stern Task for Stern Women

There is nothing in the epidemic of SPANISH INFLUENZA to inspire panic.

There is everything to inspire coolness and courage and sacrifice on the part of American women.

A stern task confronts our women--not only trained women, but untrained women.

The housewife, the dietitian, the nurses' aide, the practical nurse, the undergraduate nurse and the trained nurse herself-- all of these are needed.

Humanity calls them
Lives depend upon their answer

Capable, though untrained hands, can lighten the burden of the trained ones. There are many things intelligent women can do to relieve the situation, working under the direction of competent nurses.

Will you help do some of them ?
Will you enroll for service Now ?

If possible, apply personally at the New York County Chapter of the American Red Cross, 389 Fifth Avenue. Come prepared to fill out an enrollment blank like that printed below.

To physicians and to the nurse-employing public this appeal is made:

Unless it means life or death, please release for service all nurses attending chronic cases. Physicians should not employ nurses as office or laboratory assistants during this emergency.

Sample Enrollment Blank	
Last name.................. ....First name	
Residence.. ..Phone	**Nurses' Emergency Council,**
Business address.............. .... Phone	Lillian D. Wald, Chairman
Will serve (Hours)......................Days..................Weeks......................	Parmelia Doty, Exec, Secretary,
Occupation	
Will serve as volunteer..........................Will serve for pay.........	

Volunteers Responded Everywhere

No Passengers without Masks

White Wings' "Protection"

Masks Required Proved Useless

Jane. The wide grin flickered off the screen, too, from Douglas Fairbanks's *He Comes Up Smiling.* And Mae Marsh, figuratively speaking, was plopped back in the circular tin container labeled *Hidden Fires.*

Saloons were restricted to customers who filled their pitchers with beer and scurried out again towards uncongested home parlors. Police lurked, ever ready to arrest those who paused for a forbidden sip at the bar, just as they were ready to apprehend the new enemy of America: the "open-faced sneezer." Archbishop Mundelein prohibited "long masses and long sermons" in his Catholic diocese, and decreed that church windows — no matter how frosty the outside temperature — must be kept open. Landlords were threatened with jail if they did not provide "adequate heat." It was becoming increasingly difficult even to place a telephone call in Chicago, irrespective of whether that call was of an emergency nature. At least 20 per cent of the phone company personnel was sick.

At the University of Chicago, where nearly half of the Student Army Training Corps was ill, Dr. Louis J. Pint, a researcher, expressed the opinion that the war diet had something to do with the epidemic, especially the "curtailment of usual consumption of sugar." He suggested that the standard diphtheria antitoxin was an "absolute specific" for the flu. In South Chicago, Mrs. Ann Olds Woodson, with no pretense whatsoever to medical knowledge — who would not know *Gray's Anatomy* from Blackstone's *Commentaries* — nonetheless wrote to the War Department:

> Take two or three large, ripe but fresh red peppers of the hot variety (not the sweet variety), chop fine, put them in an open stew pan with plenty of water to cook them — set on the stove and boil nicely for an hour or more, or two hours would be better, keeping enough water to prevent their burning or getting dry.

Have outside windows and doors closed, or mostly so, the object being to permit the vapor to permeate all the air of the living apartments that the patient may inhale this impregnated air as strongly as he can take of it for the time stated above. This will cause a looseness of the cold and a coughing and sneezing. . . . Either it kills the germs of disease or causes the system to throw it off.

In some cases, a second treatment might be needed.

In Omaha, sweltering in an unseasonable hot spell, Health Commissioner Manning asserted: "The viciousness of the germs is being worn off . . . the germs, you might say, are losing strength." However, the caprice of the "germs" had fooled other doctors of stature at least equal to Dr. Manning's. The next day he was compelled to announce that the incidence was again on the increase and that last week's sixty deaths probably would be exceeded in the next seven-day period. "The epidemic comes in waves," he declared. "Today there is a great improvement. Tomorrow, the improvement may continue. Then, we may expect worse conditions."

Perhaps the blistering weather had something to do with the rise, others speculated. Whatever the factor, or factors, Dr. Manning decided to ban all public gatherings. He urged store and factory workers to wear masks and not sit close to one another. The city's packing plants, major suppliers of tinned beef for the Army and Navy, were shorthanded by at least 30 per cent due to illness.

If the flu was frustrating to Army quartermasters, it was doubly so to those in high echelons. Brigadier General H. L. Laubach in charge of Camp Custer, Battle Creek, Michigan, was among their number. Distraught by the 11,350 sick soldiers and the 537 deaths in his command, General Laubach fell back on one of the oldest bludgeons in military tradition: the court-martial. He threatened to bring officers summarily to trial who were "lax" in the camp's losing fight with the epidemic. He was unable to explain what he meant or even to prepare a list of suspects who might have permitted the microbe ingress through the armed sentries and barbed wire.

Camp Dodge, Iowa, was hurt even more fundamentally than Custer. The Army, the Red Cross and the Public Health Service continued to rush nurses into Camp Dodge, where the mortality had increased forty-fold in two weeks' time to eighty victims a day. Now there were five hundred nurses at the Iowan encampment, housed in the library and in the post theater, with cots spread even upon the stage. Half the number of barracks had been converted to hospital wards.

The flame of the disease appeared to be flickering out in Grand Rapids, in Indianapolis, in Birmingham, and even in Atlanta, where it was planned to reopen the schools and theaters. In Louisiana, however, there were a quarter of a million cases. New Orleans was closed and shuttered. And the total affected in Ohio was nearing one hundred thousand. All the coal mines had been reduced to a fraction of their normal tonnage, and factories were half or even one-third staffed.

Detroit now increased the fine for spitting to fifty dollars. At Ann Arbor, University of Michigan students were ordered to wear masks at all times under penalty of suspension.

In Pennsylvania, State Health Commissioner Royer threatened to put Scranton under martial law if the saloons did not obey the padlocking. There were a third of a million ill in Pennsylvania. Armories in the western portions of the state were being turned into hospitals. Philadelphia, with 711 deaths in the past twenty-four hours, remained a crucible of pestilence. The city's mortality from all causes was 700 per cent above normal.

In Buffalo, New York, two thousand schoolteachers, with no classes to conduct, commenced a house-to-house check to ascertain how many were in need of help. In a twenty-four-hour period, seventy-nine deaths had been reported. The figure, however, was approximately one sixth the rate in New York City, where Dr. Copeland continued reluctant to tag the epidemic "serious." He preferred to label it "widespread." Theaters remained open, even though the illness of many actors and actresses had perforce rung down curtains. "I'm keeping my theaters in as good condition as my wife keeps our home," Dr. Copeland boasted. "And I can vouch that is perfectly sanitary." Nonetheless, the mayor was sufficiently concerned to order city engineers to start digging graves. There was evidence that the specter of unburied dead was commencing to haunt New York, even as it had other cities.

In Newark, Health Officer Craster asserted that "influenza is not a very serious disease in itself." Complicated by the refugees from the Morgan explosion, nonetheless, the health prospects in the sprawling Newark area were not good. There were a thousand new cases of influenza daily, accounting for nearly one fifth of the state-wide total.

Altogether, more than 100,000 were ill in New Jersey; Connecticut counted 110,000 sick; Virginia twice that number.

The mounting toll from the epidemic among both military and civilian populations was testimony in itself to the inability of anything — or anyone — to cope with the disease. Dr. Gorgas was in Europe, touring the front lines; in fact, General Pershing's top medical man of the A.E.F., Major General Merritte W. Ireland, would assume the office of the Surgeon General by the end of October. Nonetheless, assistant surgeons general continued the work of amassing totals, and they were disquieting ones: 10,741 Army dead to date.

Far from their home shores, a large group of United States Navy men were becoming aware of the flu's presence. Aboard the armored cruiser U.S.S. *Pittsburgh,* anchored off Rio de Janeiro, Captain George B. Bradshaw USN had read the morning sickness report with considerable displeasure. Not only were there ninety-five cases of influenza smoldering within his command but during the night one crewman, Seaman E. L. Williams, had died.

This news was especially disquieting to the captain, who well knew that his stern discipline had earned him the sobriquet "Blackjack Bradshaw." He also was aware, though it was an even more bitter pill, that this wartime home for twelve hundred officers and enlisted men was commonly known as the "U.S.S. *Madhouse.*" And when it came to his attention, as it sometimes did, that a member of his command spoke of serving as "an inmate aboard Blackjack Bradshaw's floating squirrel cage," he boiled inwardly with impotent rage. To stop such talk was akin to shadow-boxing. All Captain Bradshaw could do was to keep enforcing rules calculated to maintain a "smart ship," even though he had long since despaired of skippering a "happy ship."

At the moment because of germs, it appeared that he could not even boast a "clean ship." Surely if the accursed epidemic continued at the present rate of acceleration, his would not even be "a good fighting ship." Their mission had been a curious one: patrolling these South Atlantic waters to intercept German agents moving between Spain and neutral Argentina. In effect, it meant long periods in port, awaiting orders, like a chained hunting dog whose master hasn't determined the scent upon which to unleash him.

The men, inevitably, grew restless. Whether the *Pittsburgh* had ever been a madhouse or not, the crew was now turning it into one. In the past ten days, Rio itself had been swept by flu, thus denying even shore leave to the sailors of the American warship. Spas such as the boisterous Highlife Club (which was pronounced "Heegie-Liffey") shone from across the mirror-like harbor waters like some electrified Lorelei, as unattainable now to the American sailors as a phantasm springing from their thwarted desires. In marked contrast to United States Navy precautions, Rio had not closed its public places. Rather, its frenetic pace was stepped up even as the citizenry dropped dead with ever-increasing frequency.

It was obvious to Lieutenant Ellis M. Zacharias, gunnery officer on the *Pittsburgh,* who had already had the grippe, that the Brazilians were attempting literally to "drench" the epidemic by drinking "inordinate quantities" of rum. The cafés kept open until dawn blushed behind Sugar Loaf Mountain. The throb of sultry music and occasionally high-pitched, suggestive laughter drifted down the Praia do Flamingo and across the stillness of Guanabara Bay to the anchored *Pittsburgh.* Some bluejackets did not see how they could endure the torment one more day.

Indeed, for what had so many of them slavishly memorized the "key" Portuguese phrases? *"Moco!"* would surely fetch a waiter, the little book promised, as *"Cerveja"* should bring him back with a bottle of beer; and, by and by, the question *"Onde um banho quente?"* no doubt would elicit directions to the bathroom. Now what good was this linguistic knowledge?

Captain Bradshaw, however, was past fretting over strong drink, music, dancing girls or wasted application to a strange language. He knew that he had to be prepared for every contingency, and his complement included but three surgeons.

"Lowry!" he finally called, after privately debating the matter for some hours. "Lowry!"

His executive officer, Lieutenant Commander F. J. Lowry, waiting in the captain's anteroom, arrived on the run.

"Send ashore, Mr. Lowry!" he snapped, now more formal. "We've got to buy some coffins. But just two coffins! Can't have the God-damn things all over the ship if the God-damn flu peters out . . . Can we?"

14

There has been a tremendous rush for camphor in drug stores. Being a drug clerk, I felt a little inquisitive and asked customers what they were going to do with it. One of them said she would put it in a little bag and keep it to her chest. Another told me that she would break it into small pieces and scatter it in her clothes. By so doing, they would be immune from the epidemic. . . . After a little pondering I came to the conclusion that the person who advised the use of camphor in such a form is an imbecile.

DR. PHILIPPE SAINTE-MARIE, internist at a large emergency hospital in Montreal, was far from an imbecile. Yet he found that camphor could be put to good use. He administered it as a mouthwash and also injected 10 c.c.'s of it hypodermically every six hours. "It saved many who became cyanosed, with temperatures of 104°F., pulse 110-130 . . . unconscious and dying," he reported in the Boston *Medical and Surgical Journal.*

Nonetheless, where skill and intelligence were not available, superstition, quackery and primitive fears were the often unwitting henchmen of the germ itself. And Dr. C. E. Fisher of Sterling, Colorado, had encountered these elements at their worst. Dispatched by the Public Health Service, his mission was to treat the predominantly Latin population of Torrance County, New Mexico. In a dual role of medical man and policeman, he must enforce rules against mingling with the sick and placard, in Spanish, those houses where the fever raged. And there were many. At Manzano, built at the very base of 10,000-foot-high Osha Mountain, there were two hundred flu cases a day. At this rate, everyone in tiny Manzano would be sick in another two days. Families had been obliterated to the last member. In one cemetery, Dr. Fisher counted twenty-four freshly dug graves.

The physician's continuing challenge was how to communicate with these silent, stoic people who practiced such rites as burning and scourging themselves. "Huddled crowds" met him "everywhere, on the street corners and in the stores," watching him, quietly, fearfully, as though they could not resolve whether he had brought the curse upon their community or represented salvation.

A thousand miles to the east, an unusual ceremony was being solemnized in St. Louis. As the clock struck twelve, Jacob E. Meeker, forty-year-old member of the Missouri delegation to the House of Representatives, was married to his secretary, Mrs. Alice V. Redmon.

It was a warm, still evening, barely punctuated by the traffic on adjoining South Kings Highway, the location of the Jewish Hospital where the marriage was taking place. Circuit Court Judge Vital W. Garesche stood by Representative Meeker's bed to read the vows as doctors and nurses were witnesses. Everyone, including the bride, wore hospital gowns and masks. The groom himself, his face almost obscured by a mask, breathed laboriously, virtually unable to repeat the solemn sentences.

The Congressman had journeyed from Washington the week

before to check on the need for additional masks at Jefferson Barracks, when he was stricken with the flu. Meeker and Mrs. Redmon, a widow with four children, had for many months been engaged, but there was always something concerned with the war or politics that caused them to postpone their wedding plans.

On Tuesday afternoon, October 15, Dr. W. H. Fuchs, the Congressman's physician, was forced to make a grave decision. He summoned Mrs. Redmon to his office and told her that Jacob Meeker might not survive another twenty-four hours. *If* she wished to marry him, he added, he would aid in arrangements with the hospital. They had been wed but seven hours when Jacob Meeker became the first Congressman to succumb to the epidemic.

The disease also reached into a jail cell in Topeka, Kansas, this Wednesday dawn where Frank Lewis, mail train bandit and policeman murderer, cheated the hangman by dying of influenza.

In Pittsburgh, meanwhile, Dr. Karl Schaffle of the Pennsylvania Health Commission called for more doctors, more nurses, more volunteers in all classifications as the steel mills were threatened with closing. "Influenza here is inevitable," he stated, "but we can prevent pneumonia . . . Influenza in an epidemic wave is coming solidly across the state." He urged more tent hospitals where the patients "can have air and sunshine."

Complicating the doctors' efforts was the shortage of medical supplies and even of drugstores. According to B. E. Pritchard, secretary of the Western Pennsylvania Retail Druggists Association, prescription business had increased nearly 800 per cent in two weeks. The only way some druggists could avoid saturation of effort was to close their shops several hours each day to catch up on back orders. The possibility of being unable to obtain medication further frightened even the healthy among the population. Men and women, otherwise able, stayed away from their jobs, gripped with unreasoning dread.

Health and police officials, at the same time, found their own troubles compounded by two recalcitrant extremes: churches and saloons. Constant violations of the closing law in both categories were growing so flagrant that Judge Thomas D. Carnahan finally barked that he'd lock up "both ministers and bartenders" if necessary to enforce the dual ban.

H. P. Drake, a state health department sanitary engineer, pronounced conditions in the coal mining districts "desperate beyond belief." He spoke, for example, of one family, that of William Lucas of Natrona, in which mother, father and their four children were all abed with the flu. A neighbor, William Watson, his wife and two of their children were similarly stricken, while one daughter had diphtheria.

Pennsylvania was sick with more than one third of a million cases. Ten thousand had died there in less than two weeks. It was the most severely affected state in the union.

It was particularly a paradox that death in one of its most terrible forms should arrive with the splendid autumn. Around Clearfield, colors were at their most dazzling, as the maples paled into amber and the oak and chestnut leaves turned from green to russet, hurried along by the first frosts. The orchards bordering the dirt road leading north from Clearfield towards Mount Joy were ablaze with the reds and yellows of Smoke House and Baldwin apples. They hung heavily from the trees and bedecked the ground with a lush, careless artistry. High overhead, the geese honked as they winged southward. Old men and old women looked upward and shook their heads sadly, knowing full well that another season was ending and winter would soon return to the earth.

This fall, the sound of footsteps over crisping leaves had

somehow funereal overtones. Missing was the cry of children going to class. With schools closed, most of the youngsters were kept at home by their fearful parents. Even those areas of familiarity and relaxation, the ice-cream parlors, had lost their pleasant, familiar aspect. Chairs and tables had been removed to make patronage as brief — and unpleasant — as possible.

Only one citizen, Benjamin Chase, found balm in this, as he snapped, "It will put a stop to spooning of maids and misses and silly swains wading through their first paroxysms of calf love." The Clearfield *Progress,* in a front-page story, noted:

> The influenza epidemic throughout Clearfield County and this section of the state is becoming much more serious than the general public seems to recognize. From every section comes the same story of the rapid spread of the disease, and the health authorities are adopting much more stringent regulations to combat the disease.
>
> The epidemic which first broke out along the Atlantic coast is now rapidly making its way west. Every section of Clearfield County is affected now and in many places the condition is serious. . . .
>
> During the past 24 hours at least 10 deaths were reported. The undertakers were so busy last evening that they did not have the time to check up their records and no dependable list was obtainable.
>
> Out at No. 2 shaft the disease is gaining quite a foothold. There were two deaths there yesterday, a man and his wife, and several other cases are reported as very serious.
>
> The meeting of the local health board in the council chamber last evening was attended by about 20 citizens who insisted the health authorities take the most drastic steps toward regulating the town and combating the spread of the disease.
>
> It was suggested and strongly insisted upon that the town be absolutely quarantined against travel of any description and people be forbidden to either leave or enter. . . .
>
> Acting Health Officer McDivitt will be given a saddle horse

to enable him to patrol the town, enforce the quarantine and break up all congregations of people.

Officer McDivitt, astride his charger, perhaps could disperse gatherings of people, intimidate customers away from the back doors of otherwise locked-up saloons, and even assure an "open funeral" on the porch of the deceased's home. But the flu microbes did not scare easily, as commanding generals who fancied armed sentries and courts-martial an antidote were learning to their chagrin.

The disease was sweeping Clearfield, as it had swept other towns and cities farther east, irrespective of whether people gathered or cowered behind shuttered windows and bolted doors. Judge Joseph E. Phillips had now established a second emergency hospital in the high school building, a large brick structure just across the river and facing a bridge which led to the center of the town. To be certain its capacity would not be exceeded, the jurist also ordered six large Army tents to be spread upon the school's lawn.

The Reverend Mr. Reeve was already a regular visitor to the newest hospital, even as he was to that of Elizabeth Clees farther up the river on Old Town Road. He had developed a procedure by which he hoped to assure his own immunity — carrying two small bottles of alcohol with him. One was for washing his hands, the other, a weaker solution, for gargling.

The saddest part of a minister's duties was projecting itself more and more into the forefront of Mr. Reeve's day: funerals. This afternoon, for example, he officiated at the last rites for Edith Viberg, who had died at Camp Lee, Virginia. In Dubois, two other nurses succumbed to the flu, Miss Helen Bacon and Miss Mary Flood.

The lack of physicians in sizable Clearfield County seriously hampered what treatment there was to be given. There were but five — to care for a population of 100,000. One was Dr.

Richard Williams, at nearby Houtzdale, the brother of Elizabeth Clees. As a county coroner, his duties, like those of the ministers, were magnified and rendered all the more lugubrious by the epidemic. Dr. Williams was so busy in his own section that he was unable to drive even the twenty miles to Clearfield to see his sister and perhaps help with her continuing ministrations.

Industry and transportation both were crippled. Coal production this week was down by 100,000 tons, mutely demonstrating the futility of Fuel Administrator James R. Garfield's latest edict: "Let there be no shortage of coal!"

At Plymptonville, New York Central railroad personnel based there were reported "badly hit" by the infection. The "eternal vigilance" that Borough Solicitor Urey's flu committee kept calling for was surely needed. The question it posed, however, became increasingly vexing: Was it already too late?

Health officials in Philadelphia were beginning to think so. As they closed out a week's records on Friday, October 19, they were faced with figures that were not to be denied: there had been 5270 deaths in the city the past week, all but some six hundred of them attributable to influenza and pneumonia or a combination of the two. Translated, this meant Philadelphia was registering a death rate of over 156 per thousand — more than 700 times what was normal. Dr. Cairns, chief of the board of health, announced that 10,000 shots of vaccine were on stock at City Hall, and "every doctor in the city is welcome to a supply."

There was an attendant problem in Philadelphia: convalescence. How to treat the increasing thousands who were recovering from the flu? Well over 100,000 persons who had contracted the fever were now struggling back to health. Recuperation, doctors knew, would be extremely tedious; it might be months before some of those who had been hurt most cruelly would be out of danger of possible heart, kidney, or nervous disorders, or even of pulmonary tuberculosis. Emergency hospitals now began converting one or more wards for convalescence. The Philopatrian Club, for example, designated its billiard room for this special purpose.

In Washington, where the daily deaths had just increased from eighty-three to ninety-one and the new cases to 1500 for the same twenty-four-hour period, the *Evening Star* reported that "strong hope is held out by the District health authorities and the physicians in charge of the cooperative work of the public health service that the high record of the influenza has been reached." The special health administrator, Dr. Mustard, as well as Commissioner Brownlow, were both in bed, sick. Their condition, however, was not critical. Dr. Fowler, the health officer and sole ranking city official still on his feet, said a complete quarantine was "uncalled for." However, he ordered twenty-five tent hospitals to be pitched on the Mall and requested "more automobiles, more drivers." By nightfall, the canvas hospitals were up and manned by Army nurses and soldiers.

"In a way I am optimistic after looking over the influenza conditions in the city," he added. "I believe or at least hope that the crest of the contagion has been reached . . . However, I am not to be understood as saying that we have mastered the situation."

Ruth McKay, a nineteen-year-old War Department clerk, was one of many volunteer helpers who could agree that the situation was far from "mastered." She would finish her shift at 4 P.M., then walk to the nearby 500-bed emergency hospital on Virginia Avenue.

One afternoon Ruth would be smoothing the bedsheets for a new patient. The next afternoon she would find the patient replaced by yet a new one. Finding it "unbelievable the way they went," she was especially awed by how many elderly women were brought in.

> They looked like skeletons [she observed]. Almost none recovered, and this was also true of pregnant women.
>
> Some families we almost had to fight off at the doors, to keep them out of our way, and from breathing the air needed by the sick people. The Italian families persisted in bringing fruit, wine, cakes — baskets splitting with food which the patients couldn't possibly eat.

It was a punishing routine which Ruth had set for herself. She was up at 6 A.M. She did not go off duty until 10 o'clock at night. Promptly at that hour, there would be a familiar chug-chug and rattle on Virginia Avenue. It was signal enough without the intrusion of a horn. Arthur King, her fiancé, had arrived in his Model T. The young wholesale grocer from Alexandria would then take Ruth to her apartment halfway across the city on Clifton Street. It was only a few blocks from where Dr. Leake, in charge of one of the three clinical units into which the enlarged and relocated hospital was divided, himself lived; yet he would often have only four hours of the twenty-four for sleep.

Ruth was too tired these nights to stop for a glass of milk or a plate of scrambled eggs en route — certainly to tarry at Haines Point along the Potomac, the city's most picturesque and popular lovers' lane. Chomping on a cigar, his bowler hat jammed on his head, King would scowl in disapproval as he drove, and dourly observe: "This is one hell of a romance!"

Doctors, especially the surgeons general, were more than ready to add that it was "one hell of an epidemic." The Army announced there had been 288,331 cases in camps to date, and more than 14,000 deaths. The new case rate per week in the Army was down by two thousand, although fatalities continued on the increase. This led a spokesman for the Surgeon

General to announce: "It is believed the present report will show that the crest has been reached so far as the number of new cases of influenza is concerned and that the subsequent reports will show a rapid decline."

However, to be certain that the somewhat smoldering fires did not flare again, an order was published simultaneously forbidding all furloughs and leaves of absence. The objective was as well "to prevent the spread of influenza through civic communities."

And Chief of Staff Peyton March again advised Pershing, who was continuing to burn up the transatlantic cables with demands for men and more men:

> Epidemic has not only quarantined nearly all camps but has forced us to cancel or suspend nearly all draft calls. Continued shipments are consequently draining reservoir of men in this country. Only a few thousand replacements for November are in service . . .

15

Another type of case became totally unconscious hours or even days before the end, restless in his coma, with head thrown back, mouth half open, a ghastly pallor of the cyanosed face, purple lips and ears — a dreadful sight.

DR. JOHN F. HOGAN, assistant commissioner of health in Baltimore, had seen too many of this "type" and others, too. He was wearied of bodily illness and appalled at death in such unseemly magnitude. Moreover, the physician who had fled from fear-crazed women earlier in the month was himself sick. In fact, he had been stricken with no warning. He remembered lurching down St. Paul Street late the past evening toward his apartment at the intersection of Preston. He was singing and reciting verses of poetry he had thought long since forgotten. At the entrance to his apartment the doorman looked at him and blanched.

"Are you all right, Dr. Hogan?" he asked with concern.

"I'm okay," the assistant commissioner replied, spitting blood as he spoke. He was sufficiently rational to dose himself with aspirin and quinine before he went to bed.

About 11 A.M. the telephone rang. Dr. John D. Blake, the commissioner of health, was calling.

"You talk pretty well for a dead man, John," Dr. Blake allowed, with a note of bemused amazement.

"What do you mean?" Hogan answered.

"You buy a newspaper and see!"

Dr. Hogan sent out for an early edition of the *Evening Sun* and there was his own brief obituary, somberly stating that "he was attacked by the malady last night." He next called up a friend at the paper, one of mingled depths of religion and superstition. Hogan so shocked the man on the other end of the wire that the latter commenced: "Our Father who art in Heaven . . ."

New York's death toll, nearly eight hundred in the past twenty-four hours, had exceeded that of Philadelphia. Thus the largest city in the nation had also become the greatest hotbed of influenza. Dr. Copeland, however, cautioned not to think of the epidemic as "serious," but rather, "let's call it widespread." The health commissioner at the same time reported "glorious news" from the Public Health Service to the effect that the national incidence of new cases was decreasing. Still defending his position in not padlocking the city, he told reporters:

> Had we adopted a universal order with respect to the closing of theaters and picture shows we should then logically have closed every department store, every office and factory, every restaurant and cabaret show, and every club. The disease is one which is spread to a large degree by contact in the home, and even if we went through some Utopian method of policing to confine every person to his or her home, it is doubtful whether the epidemic could be measurably diminished.

At 21 East 40th Street, however, an organization voted its own closing. A solemn little group of men and women volunteers conducted a noisy but final ceremony consisting of smashing several thousand German gramophone records on the hard tile floor of the leased store premises. They then bade one another farewell and walked out of the front door for the last time.

The National Phonograph Records Recruiting Corps had gone out of business. The government's ill-starred "Everybody Sing" campaign had croaked to a husky whisper. No one wanted to risk coming close enough to another person to harmonize. Few had the heart any longer to crank up their Victrolas for the dubious balm of Madame Schumann-Heink. The six-hundred-million-dollar music and concert industry in America was silent now. Not even light arias or operettas could cause people to forget the dirge that echoed across the land.

Mayor John F. Hylan, with possibly nothing more to go on than rumor, issued a public warning against medical overcharging. He would, he threatened, "advertise" any unethical doctors "to the world, and pin upon them a badge of shame that will last longer than their ill-gotten gains."

Dr. Martha Wollstein, meanwhile, continued to seek the cause of the blanketing epidemic.

> We may [she wrote] accept the wide prevalence of the so-called influenza bacillus as established and admitted and then proceed to the next and more important because essential question of the relationship of the bacillus to the symptom-complex influenza. Except in epidemic periods this symptom-complex is not so definite as to enable a sure and prompt diagnosis of influenza to be made.

Looking at the situation from a somewhat more elemental standpoint, Dr. Edward D. Wisely of New York's Draft Board 187 wrote the Surgeon General of the Army: "I believe that the high death rate from influenza is caused by acidosis. Getting happy results by administration of 30 grains bicarbonate of soda every four to six hours, 30 grains citrate of potash every four to six hours, alternating. It is worth a trial period." The Surgeon General's office apparently did not think it was. The letter was filed.

Newark counted 107,000 cases, with a seemingly hopeless acceleration rate of 15,000 additional each day. Mayor Charles P. Gillen issued a machine-gun spurt of orders which inspired his political opponents to charge he had "lost his head." They were unquestionably topped by one prohibiting all future influenza news to be issued from any office other than his own. Thereupon he confounded every resident of the big city by revoking the quarantine. In turn, the State Board of Health at once revoked Gillen's own revocation, asserting angrily: "The epidemic still prevails in the city of Newark to a very alarming extent." There were, the board pointed out, fifty-six or more deaths in Newark every twenty-four hours.

Again the mayor's foes gleefully joined the battle of authority, charging that Gillen had revoked the orders because he himself was weary of "sneaking through the back doors of saloons." The state's overriding action was "hysterical" and also "absurd," an infuriated Gillen countered. He told the saloons, theaters, and other establishments to go ahead and open up anyhow. In the *Newark Evening News* there was a notice indicative of the times: "The whist which was to have been held tomorrow at the home of Mrs. Lula S. Smith, 208 N. Nineteenth Street, East Orange for the benefit of the Roseville Chapter No. 48, O.E.S., has been postponed."

The engagement of Miss Margaret Colie of Prospect Street, East Orange, to Ensign Theodore Burnham Van Nest of Litchfield, Connecticut, was announced. The wedding, however, would not be held. Ensign Van Nest had died that very day of flu aboard a transport bound for France.

And in her Livingston Street apartment a Newark resident,

Mrs. Anna Padolek, turned on the gas jets — and thereby brought to an abrupt end her grieving over the recent death from influenza of her husband.

In Philadelphia, 650 died in one day, a carnage which almost lent veracity to a recent Berlin claim that dead were "heaped" in American streets. Other areas of Pennsylvania fared little better. In Clearfield, the sight of the black-paneled wagon, drawn by a plodding old mare, was all too familiar. It was the hearse from Leavy, the undertaker.

Sunday, October 20, was rainy, after a moonlit night. Out past Wolf Run and along Mount Zion Road, Ella Fulton, with her girl friends, had been out gathering apples. Later they would take the well-ripened fruit to the cider presses, as another part of a pleasant autumnal custom. While Ella, the stenographer who was being courted by Borough Solicitor Urey, was collecting apples, Kim Clees was driving one of his demonstrator Franklins to Tyrone, thirty miles to the east, on an emergency errand. Clearfield had exhausted its meager stock of oxygen. However, the Pennsylvania health commission had located several tanks and shipped them from Harrisburg to Tyrone.

The clarity of the night, however, could not compensate for the rutty, winding roads nor the leisurely pace of the sedan. Unlike a Stutz or a Packard, this sedan had not been designed for speed. With all his personal dedication to the mission, it was nearly 3 A.M. on Sunday before Kim guided his Franklin noisily back into Clearfield, bearing the life-giving cargo.

A few hours later, while it was barely light, Cecil Bloom, the druggist, was awakened by loud voices. His apartment at Second and Cherry Streets was located in the rear of the telephone exchange. He finally realized that he was overhearing a conversation between the Clearfield operator and her counterpart in Wilkes-Barre.

143

"Mrs. James," the woman kept saying, "Mrs. James" — until Bloom realized what the two were talking about. Edgar James, an enormous man in his late twenties, had died of the flu. Edgar, who worked for the CBC Coal Company, and sang bass in Mr. Reeve's choir, had helped Bloom all week carrying medicine to Nurse Clees's emergency hospital. Friday he had confided that he did not feel well. On Saturday he told the druggist he was worse. Even so, Bloom had no premonition of his friend's sudden passing, and, as he struggled to wake up, he later said, he had the feeling, he'd "been hit over the head."

A slow, cold drizzle was beginning to fall on Clearfield this Sunday morning, as damper to the brilliance and beauty of the moonlit night. Another day of suffering, of fear and, for some, of loss was commencing. In the city room of the *Progress*, a reporter chronicled the dreary story:

The influenza epidemic in Clearfield has reached the dangerous stage without question and nothing but the most careful observance of all the requirements of the health authorities will avoid a serious epidemic.

The disease was first discovered in Clearfield two weeks ago last Saturday and since that time has slowly penetrated to all parts of the town, very many of the cases developing among people whose business or occupations called them out of town and into other infested communities. Accordingly during every day of the intervening two weeks there were cases of the disease developed locally from almost every section of the town.

On Sunday evening there were 31 houses under quarantine in the town while 11 patients were being treated at the emergency hospital. Eight persons had already been discharged from that institution cured after the disease had run its course.

The disease developed rapidly yesterday, some 15 cases being reported by the physicians while it is believed that there are many more than that number where no doctor has been called and home remedies are being applied. It is from these latter cases the chief danger arises because the disease is so virulent that where a case develops in a household it invariably attacks every member thereof. This is demonstrated locally by the fact that in many instances there are as high as five and six cases in one home at the same time. . . .

Many New York Central railroad men are developing the disease and this is attributed to their traveling in and out of the different towns along the line where the disease is raging. One local physician informed us last evening that a N.Y.C. tieup here would not surprise him much from his personal knowledge of the situation.

Mrs. R. K. Clees, who had been in charge of the emergency hospital, was ordered to bed by her physician yesterday and it is feared she has contracted the disease. Mrs. Clees has worked very hard and had everything in fine shape at the hospital and her illness at this time is in the nature of a calamity.

At the present time the nursing force at the hospital is composed of three graduates and two student nurses and it is hoped to secure at least one more graduate nurse and two more students and it will then be possible to work them in eight hour shifts . . .

The influenza, it is said, will run its course in six weeks and as we are now entering the third week the health authorities feel the epidemic will reach its peak this week.

Informed that the area might expect 200,000 cases of the flu, Mayor E. V. Babcock of Pittsburgh asked the city council for $100,000 in emergency funds "for proper preventative and protective measures." Emergency hospitals, including even the Court House annex on Ross Street, were now equipped or nearly equipped in Pittsburgh and extending even to its more distant suburbs, including Washington and Waynesburg. The *Pittsburgh Press* reported:

In many sections outside Pittsburgh the construction of emergency hospitals for the care of influenza patients is going on, and the county commissioners yesterday made possible an even more widespread adoption of this plan of fighting the disease when they agreed to bear the expense of these hospitals.

In Turtle Creek an influenza hospital was built and completely equipped in 40 hours by citizens of the boroughs, aided by the Westinghouse Electric Company. The work was completed yesterday, and the building will be used for the care of some of the 3,000 persons ill in that town. At Hays yesterday the board of health and the borough council held a joint meeting and determined to turn the borough building into a hospital. There is space for 35 beds. More than 200 persons are ill in the town.

Dr. P. E. Marks, superintendent of the bureau of infectious diseases of the city, made arrangements for the equipment of the courthouse annex yesterday after it became apparent that Kingsley House would be filled up as soon as there were ambulance facilities. One hundred beds were brought in from the city home at Mayview, and others were gathered from the fire engine houses. It will be possible to accommodate 300 patients at the new building.

Major E. W. Day, commanding medical officer in this city, said last night that H. Kirke Porter has offered his home in Oakland for use as a military detention hospital, and it will be used if the need develops. Just now, in the military camps, the disease is on the wane. It also became known yesterday that the Magee Hospital, which has been in Government service since early in the month as an influenza center for soldiers, is to be taken over permanently by the war department as a base hospital, beginning November 1.

In the past three weeks, more than twenty thousand Pennsylvanians had perished from influenza or pneumonia complications. The daily fatality rate was now one thousand persons.

On what came to be known as "Black Thursday," October 17, in Chicago, 381 people in the city died of the flu and more than 1200 more sickened. The rate had galloped ahead by 20 per cent over the preceding day. Of the two thousand patients treated in the Cook County Hospital during the past five weeks, 642 had died. Most of them were between the ages of twenty-five and thirty. The worst, according to Dr. A. Augustus O'Neill, chairman of the city's emergency committee, was yet to arrive. He predicted that "the coming week will be the most serious in the history of the epidemic." He urged, among other measures, "Let the women wear gauze masks under their veils." Health authorities saw fit to republish rules governing burial:

> There shall be no public church or chapel funerals held in Chicago over any body dead from any disease or cause whatsoever.
>
> No wakes or public gatherings of any kind shall be held in connection with these bodies.
>
> No one except adult relatives and friends not to exceed 10 persons in addition to the undertaker, undertaker's assistants, minister and necessary drivers shall be permitted to attend any funeral.
>
> No dead body shall be taken into any church or chapel for funeral services in connection with such body during the period of the present epidemic.

It was uncomfortably reminiscent of similar provisions as related by Defoe hundreds of year ago:

> That the burial of the dead by this visitation be at most convenient hours, always either before sun-rising or after sun-setting, with the privity of the church-wardens or constable and not otherwise; and that no neighbours nor friends be suffered to accompany the corpse to church, or to enter the house visited, upon pain of having his house shut up or be imprisoned.

The staffs of nursing and charity organizations, including Jane Addams and her Hull House workers, concentrated their efforts on the city's districts of squalor. And there were many.

147

The ghetto [wrote Mary E. Westphal, superintendent of the Visiting Nurse Association of Chicago] was a hotbed of influenza and pneumonia. People watched at the windows, at the doors, then beckoned us to come in, although our gowns and masks frightened some.

On one of the coldest, rainiest days which we had, the nurse met on the sidewalk in front of a home, an 8-year-old boy, barefooted and in his nightdress. She quickly saw that he was delirious and coaxing him back into the house, she found the father sitting beside the stove, his head in his hands, two children in one bed, the mother and a two weeks old baby in another.

She questioned the man, who was nearly crazed because, as he told her, he had just given his wife, a pneumonia patient, a spoonful of camphorated oil instead of castor oil. He had been up night and day caring for the wife and children, all with temperatures above 104. His temperature at the time was 101.6.

The nurse sent for the doctor, administered to the woman, bathed all the patients and sent the youngest child to the hospital, where he died a few days later.

Four of our families lost both mothers and fathers. We tried so hard to save a 28-year-old mother of four children, with a baby 9 months old. She was pregnant and died on the 11th day.

The flu devastated human bodies, and maddened some minds. Neighbors of Peter Marrazo, a laborer who lived on South Morgan Street, could attest to the latter. Too late they heard him screaming: "I'll cure them my own way!" When they battered their way through the barricaded door of his flat, they found a terrible sight. He had slashed the throats of his wife and four children. They were dead — all except Marrazo, who had inflicted only a superficial wound upon himself.

Devastating as the flu was, it nonetheless sometimes had a way of sparing the parasites of the human race: those who preyed upon the peoples' fears, the charlatans, the profiteers.

In South Chicago, not far from the room on South Morgan Street in which Peter Marrazo had murdered his family, two flu "quacks" were dispensing a watery liquid labeled "Spanish Influenza Remedy." To attract a greater crowd, they had employed a snake charmer, complete with turban and flute. Police, frustrated for lack of more appropriate legal redress, could only order the pair to disperse. On the statute books, the two had merely violated the congregating code.

A Chicago physician, Dr. Victor D. Lespinasse, meanwhile, was appealing for blood donations from those who had recovered from influenza: "Immune blood contains antibodies, substances which help to overcome the influenza germs, of much greater value than such a serum in other diseases."

At Camp Custer, one soldier died every fifty minutes. But at Camp Taylor, Kentucky, Miss Eulalie Bourgingnon, a Briton who had nursed the wounded during the Boxer Rebellion, could at last pause for breath. "Mother" Bourgingnon, who wore the Victoria Cross and who had studied under Florence Nightingale, had herself become an angel of the flu-afflicted regions of Kentucky. She had tended the stricken miners at Keyser before being summoned for more urgent, more quantitative duties at the camp.

Now the worst had passed in that state.

In Ohio, 95,000 were ill. The *Columbus Dispatch* reported that Spanish influenza "is spreading throughout the state with no sign of abatement." Dr. E. J. Schwartz, head of Ohio's division of communicable diseases declared, in fact, that the death rate "is expected to increase considerably during the next few days." Dr. Oscar Craven, acting health officer of Cincinnati, prescribing rest, fresh air and walking, issued an order forbidding factories to blow whistles or churches to ring bells at every word of an Allied victory. This effervescent news had resulted in people dancing in the streets and otherwise congre-

149

gating in obvious invitation for the swarming germs to mingle and fraternize in even more greatly augmented tempo. The physician also urged people to desist from a craze which the epidemic had sparked: dosing themselves with inordinate quantities of aspirin, in the belief that this would prevent flu.

At Orient, Ohio, the microbe had manifested what seemed especial cruelty as it leveled 75 per cent of the state school for the feeble-minded, staff and patients, nearly three hundred men and women. Six had already succumbed. The Midwest was being battered. None could deny this unhappy fact.

Yet by late Sunday it was apparent that on Saturday, the 19th, the flu had crested in these principal cities: Washington, Baltimore, Philadelphia, Providence, Syracuse, Buffalo, Indianapolis, Memphis and Nashville. In Chicago, the infection had burned itself out some twenty-four to forty-eight hours earlier. After "Black Thursday" the rate of infection, and its toll, dropped dramatically in Chicago, as it did in the other cities on Saturday, and kept falling. Among the smaller locales which also passed a peak was, finally, Brockton, Massachusetts.

In Washington, Commissioner Brownlow could remove the remaining coffins from the Central High School playground and continue them on their interrupted consignment; Father Corrigan and his band of gravediggers could rest from their nocturnal prowling of Philadelphia's streets and alleys; and in Providence Billy Sunday could denounce sin without the spectacle of people collapsing, as if in mockery, before his eyes. . . .

16

Necropsy 3456 — Patient was admitted to Evacuation Hospital 2, October 16, 1918, with a diagnosis of acute influenza; temperature 103°F., pulse 116; respiration 24. October 17, the temperature rose to 104°F.; pulse 104; respiration 30; the temperature remained above 104°F., at times reaching 105°F.; respiration increased to 50, but the pulse rate did not rise above 104 until the day of his death when it reached 120. Death occurred October 20, 1918 at 11:30 P.M.; four days after admission. . . .

THERE WAS NO SIGN of the flu's abatement in France. No armistice appeared in prospect for death or pain. The A.E.F. hospitals, presently filled with more influenza patients than battle casualties, read like the listings of a tour itinerary in peacetime: Allery, Vittel, Contrexéville, Bazeilles, Rimaucourt, Toul, Langres, Châtillon-sur-Seine, Clermont-Ferrand, Vichy, Orléans, Tours, Limoges, Savenay, Angers, Nantes, Périgueux, Rivière, Beau-Désert, Dijon . . .

The big center at Allery was the hardest hit. There had been 2300 cases of the fever and 141 deaths. All hospitals were seriously overcrowded. The American provost marshal in Paris forbade military funerals, decreeing that casualties of the epidemic be buried, with minimum ceremony, at night. This was calculated "not to further demoralize the French populace," already tormented in addition by a suicide rate three times normal. A French soldier, Michel Corday, wrote bitterly:

> It has attacked the troops, herded together as they are, with their poor food, poor accommodation, and poor medical attention, at the front as well as in the rear. It is complicated by affections of the lungs or meningitis, often fatal. It is a kind of plague. . . . They have even called it "Spanish influenza" since the King of Spain, it appears, has had it. The name suggests the title of a dance. . . .
> . . . This epidemic has been hushed up, censored . . . it was not until the middle of October that they mentioned it, since Clemenceau's son died of it. At present, 50 soldiers are dying of it every week in a single hospital at Sens, and 1,200 people in Paris. They die in a few days, sometimes in a few hours, of suffocation. . . . In Brittany, whole families are being swept away; 500 soldiers have died in a single depot. Seaports have been especially affected. At Lyons, there are not enough hearses to go around.

In the deep dark of midnight, Major General Clarence Edwards, commanding the 26th "Yankee" Division, had quit his headquarters at Bras and was slogging through the desolation of the Argonne Forest. He drove northwestward past Montfaucon, Nantillois, Cierges, and Gesnes, finally coming to a halt before the crossroads town of Ramogne. Like its sister communities, Ramogne was a desert of rubble and roofless, shattered buildings. It was a point of reference rather than a habitation, another monument to the smashing of the Hindenburg Line.

Walking, head down, through the forward trenches lacing the leveled village's perimeter, General Edwards was accosted rather peremptorily by one of his staff.

"What," he asked his superior, "is the worst news you could receive?"

"Madame . . .?" was the general's reply, thinking that his wife, whom he called "Madame," had met with an accident.

The young officer persisted, half afraid, half unknowing how to finish something he now wished he had not started.

"That isn't it," he said bluntly. He was dog-tired. He had been without proper sleep for days during the huge Meuse-Argonne offensive. He himself realized he wasn't thinking too straight. In desperation, he handed General Edwards the clipping he had torn from the *Paris Herald*.

"It must be Bessie," the commanding officer murmured even before he cupped his hands and shone his flashlight onto the piece of paper. His only child, eighteen-year-old Bessie Edwards, had died of the flu two days previously, while working as a nurse volunteer at Camp Meade.

The general was just as preoccupied as his officers. The past few days he had been especially disturbed at the death, from the fever, of his aide, Captain N. S. Simpkins, Jr., a particular favorite.

"I was worrying about Captain Simpkins," Edwards recalled. "The night was a terrible one. The roads were almost impassable and were raked by shell fire. The nearest cable office was about 14 miles away. I spoke to some of the motorcycle dispatch riders. I told them I must send a cable. Every man volunteered. One of them rode through with the cable for Madame."

Bessie had been buried the day before, with military honors, in Arlington National Cemetery. The news had come as a climax to a grim two weeks of attrition both from enemy action and disease. As Major Emerson Gifford Taylor wrote:

"The health of the command at this time was seriously impaired by the influenza epidemic. Daily, the men evacuated for sickness reached large numbers so that the effective strength of the units was seriously impaired."

Brigadier General George H. Shelton, commanding the 51st Infantry Regiment, was in the hospital, along with other officers whom Major Taylor considered "absolutely indispensable." Bad weather, a daily torment of rain and mist, increased the misery and the susceptibility to all ailments. Taylor took especial note of "the appalling state of the ground where the troops were forced to live and seek shelter. Flooded dugouts, hillsides which were merely quagmires, broken roads, great difficulty in providing or procuring sufficient hot food, continually wet clothes and blankets all tended to sap the strength of the battalions posted in the gas-drenched hollows or on slopes which were swept at all hours by snipers and artillery."

Several miles southeast of the Yankee Division, the 89th was plodding ahead in the same contested wasteland of the Argonne, aiming at the major objective: Stenay and the third German defense-in-depth system, the Kriemhilde Stellung, a northerly backstop for the Hindenburg Line. With Company G of the 356th Infantry Regiment was Private John Lewis Barkley, of Holden, Missouri, who had survived the epidemic rigors of Camp Funston the past winter and spring. His good luck had also seen him unscathed through the fighting of St. Mihiel and the early phases of the Meuse-Argonne. Now, however, he wasn't feeling well and neither were his two companions, his almost inseparable buddies ever since training days in Kansas. They were Sergeant Jesse James, a husky full-blooded Cherokee Indian, and Private Mike de Angelo, a former featherweight boxer from Philadelphia.

> Jesse and I got hold of Mike [Barkley wrote in his diary concerning the past few days], and put him between us. He seemed actually to be asleep as he walked. As soon as we halted we put him to bed near the kitchen. Then I borrowed a razor and some soap, and shaved. I drank a cup of coffee to brace me up, and reported to the pill-rollers. I figured I could get by now without being sent back, and I wanted something

to put on my head. They gave me some greasy stuff, like vaseline, and I spent the rest of the day nursing Mike. Jesse had disappeared. No one had seen him since morning.

During the afternoon six or seven hundred replacements came into the camp. They were in good condition. They certainly made us look like tramps.

That evening Jesse came back. He had caught a ride on a truck to some little town. And of course he had some liquor. Several quarts of cognac, in canteens. We drank a little, gave part of it away, and saved the rest for emergencies. Jesse and Mike and I went to bed together. For the first time in days I took off my shoes. It was twenty-one days, as nearly as I could remember.

The next morning I wished I'd made it 22, my feet were so swollen. My instep was as sore as a bad tooth. I thought I'd never get my shoes on again. We were in for a pretty good hike that day, and I came mighty close to not making the grade. I'd caught cold the night before, too. I guess if it hadn't been for Jesse's cognac I'd have had to fall out by the road somewhere.

The day after that I was pretty sick. I got separated from Jesse, and we were piled into trucks and jolted all day over terrible roads. I had thought marching was as bad as anything could be. But it seemed to me now that this was worse. I was so miserable that I hoped I would die.

We billeted that night in a town by the name of Cunel. Mike and I were assigned to a cow barn. I couldn't eat any supper. I wrapped myself up in a blanket, rolled into the straw — and passed out. The next morning I was delirious. Mike went to the French family that owned the barn and told them about me.

I have misty recollections of being carried somewhere in a woman's arms. . . .

A sturdy, good-looking young woman was trying to pour some kind of hot toddy down my throat. She was the one who'd carried me into the house.

When the girl saw that I knew her, she called in the rest of the family. There was her mother — a widow — and a feeble old man who was madame's brother. The young woman was about twenty years old and had two little children.

They all seemed glad to find me awake. They brought food, and fed it to me. I had on a heavy cotton nightshirt six sizes too large for me. I asked where my clothes were, but they didn't understand a word of English.

I pulled myself up in bed and made motions as if I were putting on a coat and buttoning it. I kept saying, "Clothes," while I was doing this.

Madame got the idea first. She laughed. "Ah, clothes," she said. *"Non! Non!"*

She pushed me back onto the pillow. I was asleep almost before my head touched it.

That evening the two women bathed me as if I were a baby. I made an awful fuss at first, but it didn't do a bit of good. I'd pull the sheet up over me and they'd pull it down again and go on with their work. I gave up after a while. I was so weak the girl alone could have handled me. And, besides, it began to feel damned good!

They gave me an alcohol rub. They washed my head and put some kind of ointment on it with a white powder sprinkled over that. When this was all finished they put me into a suit of pajamas instead of the nightshirt I'd been wearing. The pajamas had belonged to one of madame's sons, who had been killed in the war. There were also two other sons who'd been killed, and one still living. He was a captain in the army.

After the bath they picked me up, wrapped a blanket around me, and put me in a big armchair in front of a fire. They placed my feet in a crock half full of hot water and something else that smelled like whisky. Then they fed me. That was the best meal I ever ate.

There was a large piece of breast meat on the plate. "Capon!" the widow said. She made motions as if she were lifting something very heavy. Then she blew her chest out and thumped it. They all laughed, and I laughed with them.

The war had taken a felicitous turn for Private Barkley. Others, such as Private Harry T. Pressly, of Clarinda, Iowa, managed to keep going in spite of mild attacks. He wrote home:

156

I got to spitting blood yesterday and today, so called on the doctor. He examined me with the stethoscope (lung and heart) and couldn't find anything wrong. He told me not to be alarmed, but to report every day and have my temperature taken. He says that as long as my temperature is normal he does not think there is anything serious. So I am evidently getting better all right.

I quit smoking until my lungs fully recover. I felt that spitting blood perhaps came from the throat and smoking would only irritate it.

The flu continued its offensive on a world-wide front, dipping here, dipping there, as though it were determined to wipe out everyone. No nation or human species was spared.

Great Britain was badly hurt. There had been 1895 deaths the past week in the "96 great towns" of the British Isles. Of this number, 761 had been recorded in London, where the General Omnibus Company and the fire brigade had been crippled. At least 1300 members of the Metropolitan Police were ill, and crime was mounting around the London docks, Whitechapel, and other slum areas. The Prince of Wales Hospital was "choked" with flu patients, while more and more schools were closing down. The London Hospital, customarily, was unequal to the emergency. Cinemas, though not shut, presented fewer screenings, having to ventilate the premises for an hour or more between performances.

In Dublin, the cobblestone streets were washed down with disinfectants. These and many other measures were tried in Spain to combat a particularly remorseless assault from the fever which bore the country's name. But nothing did any good, even as the Barcelona correspondent for the London *Times* wrote:

> The epidemic is a most serious affair, affecting the whole of Spain, and the death rate is truly awful. The patient dies in from seven hours to four days after first feeling sick. So far as

I can make out, death is always the result of a sort of broncho-pneumonia — in Barcelona the newspapers give the death roll from the disease as 300 a day, the Civil Governor states it is 600 a day, and the medical men with whom I have spoken say it cannot be less than 1,200 a day.

In places there is panic; the theaters, music halls and public restaurants are more than half empty, dancing is forbidden, and the people go about inhaling eucalyptol, creosote or whatever the prevalent essential oil may be. Funerals are working day and night and coffins are almost unobtainable. In this office of six, two are dead. If the disease really is influenza, about which I have no doubts, it is certainly the most virulent that has occurred in my lifetime.

Units of the Brazilian fleet in European waters were anchored in Spanish, English and French ports, too sick to patrol. In Norway, few people were able to leave their homes to vote in the general election. In Lapland, the nomadic tribes met the epidemic in their own fashion: the afflicted were bunched together in communal huts, kept warm by their own body heat, and fed by reindeer meat and milk shoved under the door. Surprisingly, many recovered.

Odessa, in the Ukraine, reported 70,000 cases and "many" fatalities. Sixty-two had died in Bucharest in the past two days, while in Prague and in countless German and Austrian cities soldiers were detailed to dig graves. Coffins were virtually nonexistent, as they had been for soldiers, in this wide portion of Central Europe.

Touring the Piave front in Italy, Samuel Gompers, the American labor leader, was handed news as overwhelming as that received by General Edwards. His own daughter Sadie, who was twenty-three, had died at home of the flu.

In Capetown, at least two thousand children were newly orphaned. Business was "at a standstill." Hotels, restaurants, all public buildings were closed. Tramways, postal and telegraph systems were paralyzed, and rail service had been slashed to three trains a day. Now the insatiable microbes were invading the very jungles of Africa. The corpses of baboons, which apparently possessed no resistance to the disease, were found "by the thousands" on the roads leading from Capetown and on farms.

In India, it was difficult to count the epidemic's toll. Tens of thousands of bodies had been disposed of in remote villages before health authorities arrived. "This pandemic," wrote Dr. M. C. Nanjunda Rau, of Madras, "must have been the result of some cosmic influence . . . operating on the vitality of all living things, reducing their power of resistance against disease, thus rendering them easy victims to the onslaughts of many germs. Thus this pandemic may be considered perhaps the closing era of a certain type of civilization or of a certain type of man, just as the upheavals of the earth from the effect of some geological cataclysm have marked the closing date of various geological ages."

Certainly the captains of at least three United States warships might well have thought this the "closing era" for their own little worlds afloat. The Coast Guard cutter *Seneca* dragged into Gibraltar from Plymouth, England, with only one officer well enough to stand watch — Lieutenant Charles "Red" Armstrong, the vessel's surgeon. The Navy patrol vessel *Yacona* finally moored in Boston, with 75 per cent of her complement abed. The witticism that "the ship's cook'll soon be conning her" assumed a ring of sobering truth. In Rio harbor, Captain "Blackjack" Bradshaw of the *Pittsburgh* had every reason to believe he was the principal mourner at the burial of at least a naval era. In the eight days since the first death, the "Goddamn" flu had taken a fearful toll — 58 dead aboard his ship, 647 ill, or more than half the complement.

The medical staff had been wholly unable to keep up with

the attrition, or even the morbid demands for preparation for burial. Some help was forthcoming, however, from a slow-spoken seaman from North Carolina whose father was a mortician. Forty-four men were taken ashore to the Hospital Central do Exercito, but there were no more beds available anywhere in Rio. The city, with upwards of 200,000 ill and two thousand deaths a week, had finally submitted to the epidemic. Businesses were closed. Cafés were tightly shuttered. Streets were all but deserted. The situation was not appreciably better in Buenos Aires or other South American cities.

However, the fiery scourge had quit the United States cruiser. More than a hundred of her crew, facing lengthy recuperations, were placed upon the British transport *Vauban*, New York-bound. Now there remained little to do but bury the dead.

Under a drenching sun, an honor guard of bluejackets and Marines walked stiffly, solemnly beside the long row of coffins borne on flimsy donkey carts along the broad Rua do Ouvidor. As church and mission bells tolled, the procession, with Captain Bradshaw at its head, walked on and upward, with measured tread, past the stucco residences and the sweet-smelling gardens of the Rua Ortigao. The cortege passed the picturesque Convent of San Antonio. Perched on a commanding hill, it was the resting place of the bones of the first Empress of Brazil, Dona Leopoldina de Habsburg. At last the weary and profusely sweating men stopped. They had reached their destination: the old and richly foliaged San Francisco Xavier Cemetery.

Far below, on Guanabara Bay, the colors of the *Pittsburgh* were half-masted. When her convalescent sailors were strong enough, the cruiser would limp homeward. Her war was over.

She had been put out of action as effectively as though pummeled at Jutland.

17

Obey the laws
And wear the gauze,
Protect your jaws
From septic paws.

A S OCTOBER NEARED its final week, the fickle flu, tiring of parts of the East and Midwest, concentrated belatedly on the Pacific coast. California counted more than 40,000 cases, with one fourth of them in San Francisco. The considerable number of sixty persons were now dying daily in the City of the Golden Gate, and it seemed that Billy Sunday's recent warnings of retribution were to be realized. San Francisco, he had asserted, was "going to hell so fast it ought to be arrested for speeding." Whether this was the case or not, Mayor Rolph conceded the situation was serious enough for everyone to wear face masks. He published a city-wide ordinance to that effect. And his health officer, Dr. William C. Hassler, set the fashion with an elaborate face covering.

"The snout," observed the *San Francisco Chronicle*, "extends partially, like the helmets affected by the French knights at the period of Agincourt, but it is not so protrusive as the metal muzzles. Furthermore, it is sheathed outside in gauze like the common or garden mask more usually adopted by the public."

The police wore small gauze pads over their noses and mouths, "resembling in size and contour about nine ordinary slabs of ravioli arranged in a square of three each way. Men with strong ears that set close to the head can loop these onto the same with elastic loop." There was also, for chic women, a "yashmak" or harem veil type mask.

Whatever one's taste, a mask had better be worn. "Mask slackers" could be fined $100 or even sent to jail for ten days' isolation. Nor would sects which discounted the benefits of medicine fight the ordinance. A spokesman for the Christian Science Church, Peter V. Ross, for example, asserted: "If it doesn't do any good, it certainly won't do any harm!"

As a matter of fact, the objectors to masks had a valid excuse at the moment: the Red Cross had exhausted its supply of the approved type of protective objects. And the specter of "mask profiteering" had already arisen.

Those equipped were also finding uses for which the masks were by no means intended. W. S. Tickner, a jitney driver, picked up three mask-wearing male passengers. It turned out, however, they wore the cover to foil identification, not germs. They robbed the driver at gunpoint, then unceremoniously dumped him out of his cab as they drove away, still wearing their masks, just as Mayor Rolph had decreed.

Dancing was banned in San Francisco, theaters and many restaurants were closed. Schools were padlocked, and attendance at church limited to a small percentage of the congregation. Husbands, cherishing their Sunday mornings and their newspapers, were in hearty accord.

In spite of what some considered exaggerated precautions, the disease was on the increase and people were dying: nineteen pregnant women at the San Francisco Hospital in a maternity ward of forty-two; four students at Stanford University and the campus barber, Charlie Meyers, who had counted Herbert Hoover among his clientele; servicemen at the Presidio and other Army and Navy installations.

Sometimes it struck suddenly, even as it had done in the East. Henrietta Burt, a secretary, was enjoying a bridge game one evening. "We played until long after midnight," she recalled. "When we left we were all apparently well. By eight o'clock in the morning I was too ill to get out of bed, and the friend at whose house we played was dead."

Inevitably, the people of this state reacted with suggestions as to the control of the infection. There was agitation for pumping seawater into the hydrants and flushing streets and sidewalks of San Francisco. Mayor Rolph, with his own demonstrated notions on how to keep the germs away, scoffed: "You might as well sit out and watch the changes of the moon."

E. Christenson of the same city had a specific cure: "You could destroy that disease and every disease known by sweating it off the body — 1½ hours will destroy all kinds of disease."

At Venice, California, the Al G. Barnes Circus passed through a mandatory fumigation. Animals and performers alike were subjected to an almost suffocating spray of coal tar and formaldehyde. It was reminiscent of a gas attack on the Western front. When the noxious clouds of vapor dissipated, the "Albino Girl," along with microbes, fleas and sundry vermin and insect life, had become herself a casualty. Her silvery blonde hair was once again dark brown and her light skin had reverted to an embarrassing swarthy hue.

To the north, Elizabeth J. Davies, a nurse at the "extra-cantonment" zone around Camp Lewis, Washington, reported:

> October 7 we had our first case, a mild one at American Lake, a mother of a family, but it did not spread among the

other members. Three days passed before we discovered any more but in six days cases were found in all districts and orders were given on October 18 for the closing of all schools, which cut off a medium of infection, but also a source of knowledge. The days succeeding the closing of the schools were very hard as so much time was wasted in finding the sick instead of spending it in caring for them.

Teachers were recruited. In one district five sick children were found in a house with their ill mother. Nurse Davies continued:

In one family a married daughter from Montana came to visit her home, bringing with her a three-year-old child. The mother contracted influenza, infecting her daughter, who during the attack gave birth to a boy; the young husband arrived and came down at once with the disease, each developed pneumonia; a sister came to nurse them and she developed influenza in a few hours; another sister was telegraphed for and arrived on the scene with her family of two children, and all came down; there were not enough beds to accommodate the sick.

Belatedly, the flu had detoured into Alaska — enroute to God knows what more remote spot on the earth's surface. Vilhjalmur Stefansson, arriving in Seattle from America's northernmost territory, reported that out of some three hundred Eskimos in Nome, 176 had died. Of eight Eskimos who had accompanied him back from the Arctic, five had succumbed during his stop-off in that same city. The Alaskan epidemic was not only proving that the northerly tribesmen had no resistance to the Spanish influenza but how little medical men know about the disease's mode of transmission. The invisible killer was not only scourging Nome, a wilderness crossroads, but tiny, unfrequented Eskimo villages. How was it possible?

The disease was scattered but not severe in Utah. Ogden,

with 2289 cases, was the most severely hit. Kansas City counted four or five deaths a day.

At Camp Dodge, Iowa, the bugler once again blew reveille with a carefree lilt. There was, at last, relative certainty he would be alive to sound the same brassy matins the following day. The epidemic had nearly passed. In its fiery wake were 702 soldiers dead, out of the total of ten thousand stricken, or 30 per cent of the command.

The governor of Iowa, W. L. Harding, also was recovering, even though Iowa was still suffering from scattered points of infection. In Blairstown, for example, Guilford H. Sumner, secretary of the Iowa State Board of Health, noted that one sixth of the community's population of six hundred was sick. There was no doctor within twenty-five miles.

Cincinnati, like San Francisco, seemingly was being attacked as an afterthought by the flu. There had been fifty deaths in one day. But measures were instituted. Community kitchens started cooking, for example, and Andreas E. Burkhardt, a merchant, organized a squad of two hundred men to help him scrub the city's streets.

In Columbus, suffering proportionately to Cincinnati, police-men rode the trolleys to "prevent crowding." Physicians such as Dr. Victor Heiser, regional Public Health Service director for Ohio, however, voiced the belief it was too late; the acute congestion at military camps, he believed, had already done its damage.

The soldiers had sickened in the camps or become carriers without knowing it and then spread the disease far and wide. The 81st Field Artillery, for example, which had left Fort Sill, Oklahoma, on October 19, and was now nearing New York for its November 1 sailing date on the *Aquitania*, had left its dead and dying at almost every railroad station through which the regiment had passed. Captain George C. Rogers, who had

165

left for overseas with an advance party, was the first to die from the luckless 81st. He was buried in Liverpool, England. Of the main body of the regiment, more than three hundred had contracted the fever. The first death en route was that of Lieutenant Henry G. Mobly, at St. Louis.

In Pittsburgh, the most recent twenty-four-hour toll from the flu was 144 deaths, a drop of thirty-two from the preceding day. This led health officials to speculate that the crest had been passed. However, more and more residents were wearing masks, including all the employees of the Washington Trust Company. Tent hospitals — in Curtisville, for example — were still being erected. With eloquent distrust for feint or seeming withdrawal of the attacking microbe, all Catholic charities in Pittsburgh placed their physical and personnel facilities at the disposal of the city. In Bellevue, a western suburb, the family of Alice L. Thompson, a Navy nurse, received word that she had succumbed at Naval Base Hospital No. 4, Leith, Scotland, now being ravaged by the fever.

There seemed no hint of abatement at Clearfield. Dr. Fred Howe, one of the few physicians in the county, became the latest victim, as Elizabeth Clees continued to fight for her own life. The *Progress* wrote:

> There are possibly 700 cases of the influenza in the town today and it is only reasonable to expect that the 15 per cent of cases expected will be realized, while it is possible the percentage of cases will be much higher before the epidemic has run its course.
>
> The new emergency hospital management hereby makes an appeal to the women of Clearfield to offer their services as volunteer nurses for immediate duty. The supply of trained nurses is inadequate and this appeal is to those women who while not trained nurses, have had some experience with caring for sick people. Those accepted for service will be inoculated with anti-influenza serum . . .

166

The Board of Health decided to close all business places in Clearfield at 6 o'clock Saturday evening next to avoid all possibility of people congregating or crowding together. This action was unanimously decided upon at a meeting of the health authorities held in the council chamber last evening.

At present the doctors are very greatly annoyed and interfered with in their work by anxious and curious people insisting on calling them on the phone to inquire regarding some patient's condition or to ask some silly question regarding inoculation, vaccination or other minor propositions.

Health Officer McDivitt reported at last night's meeting of the Board of Health that he had already placarded 78 different residences and as the number of cases in the different homes run from one to seven we are safe in saying there are at least 250 reported cases in the town at present.

Serious as their own epidemics appeared in any community singled out, large or small, none could now compare with that raging in New York. The last twenty-four-hour count was more than eight hundred dead. Civic functions were badly disrupted, with policemen, firemen, transit employees and trash collectors victims. Two thousand telephone operators, or 25 per cent of the staff, were ill.

And still researchers such as Dr. Martha Wollstein sought the cause. While continuing to question the generally accepted theory that Pfeiffer's bacillus was the cause of influenza, she could not arbitrarily say it was not. Tediously, patiently, she had to explore every medical bypath, though she knew 99 per cent of them would likely be dead ends.

The patients' serological reactions [she wrote] indicate the parasitic nature of the bacillus, but are not sufficiently stable and clean-cut to signify that Pfeiffer's bacillus is the specific inciting agent of epidemic influenza. They do, however, indicate that the bacillus of Pfeiffer is at least a very common secondary invader in influenza and that its presence influences the course of the pathological process.

Her colleague Dr. Peter Olitsky wrote wearily of the obstacles which strewed the path of the epidemiologist:

> The disease is transitory, the acute stage enduring for only a few days. As a rule, the patient comes to the attention of the bacteriologist when secondary invasion by ordinary bacteria has set in, which complicates, and perhaps suppresses, the primary incitant. Furthermore, epidemics occur explosively with the result that many cases may be offered for examination at about the same time and each cannot be studied in the most desirable way. Still another hindrance arises from perplexity in selecting, during widely spreading epidemics, individuals for control observation, that is, those who have not been attacked by the disease. Again, in respect to the subject of filter-passing anaerobes of the human nasopharynx, lack of a more simple, uniform and exact technique in collecting and cultivating material, and the absence of a precise taxonomy, are troublesome factors. Finally, experiments such as are made upon laboratory animals, including the lower monkeys, are hedged by impediments. Influenza is not known to occur naturally among them; hence the question arises when an experimental infection is induced as to whether it is or is not true influenza . . . many of these animals when taken from stock suffering from snuffles.

In Newark, on October 22 and 23, the theaters reopened, as Mayor Gillen continued his defiance of state health authorities. Even as there were mutterings of impeachment from the state capitol in Trenton, the lights went on at these movie palaces: the Newark Theater, "a safe picture house," where Charlie Chaplin was playing in *Shoulder Arms;* the Fox Terminal, with Theda Bara in *When a Woman Sins,* and also *Swat the Spy,* with Jane and Catherine Lee; and the Goodwin, with Harold Lockwood in *Pals First.* It would be Lockwood's last film. The handsome, popular actor had died of influenza three days previously. That week, the Boston theaters had also reopened.

Meanwhile, from all sections of the nation, opinions, theories and "cures" continued to be voiced.

"I feel sure in my soul," wrote Mrs. W. A. Field, of Socorro, New Mexico, "that it must be because last winter in a mining camp in Arizona all of a sudden a lot of the miners, about 60, took ill with this same influenza or grippe and on investigation it was found that a German sympathizer had put something in the drinking water."

Theodore Payne, of Passaic, New Jersey, seconded to the War Department: "Can it be that the prevailing epidemic of grippe or Spanish influenza in this country and particularly in the Army camps is due to some German microbe used in connection with the distribution of millions of cigarettes to our boys in camps throughout the country?"

In a syndicated health column a letter from a reader who signed himself "S.Q." was printed:

> The morning I noticed the symptoms, I drank two quarts of hot water and I started spraying my nose and throat — my diet has been milk and bran and fruit, except the hot water I drank occasionally. Each morning when my head was stuffed and throat sorest I drank two quarts of hot water and I immediately felt like a new man. On the fourth day, I was practically well.

In Atlanta, E. A. Rogers urged people to eat asafetida, and Philip Lynch, a New York broker, suggested that the dust from old books, donated to the troops, carried the disease.

Authorities in Washington continued to be increasingly dismayed by all such gratuitous advice. Surgeon General Blue issued a new warning: "The Health Service urges the public to remember that there is as yet no specific cure for influenza and that many of the alleged cures and remedies now being recommended by neighbors, nostrum vendors and others do more harm than good."

18

ON SATURDAY, October 26, a common bond was to be established between Omaha, Minneapolis, Milwaukee, Toledo, Columbus, Rochester, Albany, New York City, and Newark.

The day was unprepossessing in Omaha, where rain alternated with snow flurries. The thermometer hovered around 35°. The raw weather was made all the more bleak by the 40,000 existing influenza cases in the state and the bad news from the Food Administration. Hog prices had been pegged at $17.50 per 100 pounds, a maximum, farmers complained, which "will hardly pay for the feed they use."

An oasis of civilization in hundreds of miles of empty prairie, Omaha had been host for the past weeks to more than a hundred actors and actresses, stranded because of cancellations in other cities. Most had gone to work in emergency wards, in soup kitchens, or in the motor corps. Taking pity, the Elks Lodge No. 39 today opened its doors, inviting them to use the building as their own club.

Omaha, with all the disruption to its civic and business life, primarily meat packing, had fought heroically to keep going.

The experience of Anton Schneckenberger, a printer, was in some respects typical, in others, extraordinary. Anton was just emerging from the harrowing ordeal of playing nurse to his wife and nine sick children:

> My wife had made careful charts for each child, listing on them the medicine for each, the time of taking and a place for all kinds of records. Five took one kind of cough medicine and the other three took another kind. The charts enabled me to keep from getting the medicines mixed up.
>
> I used ice water and cloths and three ice bags at their heads and hot water bottles at their feet. From Saturday night until Tuesday noon I had only two hours rest. By the time I would reach the last, the first would want something.

While relatives supplied the food, the overworked head of the family washed all the dishes. "I kept cheerful" was his laconic explanation of how he maintained his own health and equilibrium.

In Minneapolis, two and a half inches of snow lay on the ground, and the air was very cold. The flu had claimed a thousand lives in Minnesota since the start of the epidemic and attacked 35,000 persons. There was hope the frosty temperatures would nip Minneapolis's illness, which this day reached a high thus far of 101 new cases and thirteen deaths.

There were many problems this late October, some relative to the flu, some utterly irrelevant, merely the punctuation in civic and personal existence. Chinatown, for example, with a population of two hundred, was being "cleaned up." Chinese were routed out of damp, dark cellars where they had slept like prisoners, and rehoused in cleaner, newer above-ground shelters. The suspicion was that the dungeon recesses were not so much Tong meeting places as opium parlors. The proprietor of one of them obliquely informed a reporter: "Yes, been velly, velly busy."

Politically, Minnesota's Governor J. A. A. Burnquist was under a lashing from opposition statesmen in connection with the recent fatal forest fires. He was accused of laxity in policing the woods as well as giving warning to those who lived on the fringes.

And, with winter coming, buying must continue, whatever the other distractions and disturbances. Furniture sales, now at their height, offered walnut dining suites for $149.50, spinet desks for $31.50, Stewart coal stoves "on attractive terms," and Pianola player pianos for $575.

In Wisconsin, Milwaukee was saddened this cold Saturday by the death of an eighteen-year-old dancer who used the stage name Freddye Amiot. She had appeared with the Empress Burlesque and Stock Company while her husband, Sam Mitchell, was overseas with the 306th Field Artillery. The work for Freddye was essential towards the support of one-year-old Sam, Jr. Only the day before, she had complained, "I have the funniest pain in my knees today — I can't seem to walk. I guess I've got the flu." Freddye had been ill less than twenty-four hours when she became one of Milwaukee's thirty-one flu victims this Saturday. There were 204 new cases, which was considered very high for this city. As the winds howled in from Lake Michigan, however, there were many residents who predicted "good-by flu." It seemed to them that the cold weather would kill the germs.

In Toledo, the incidence was somewhat below that of Milwaukee, but city fathers were determined to halt the epidemic before it was fanned into an inferno, as it had been in Chicago and the giant cities of the East. The heavy artillery in the medical defense of this lake metropolis consisted of sixteen dispensing stations, where citizens could be vaccinated or doctors obtain a supply of the new serum. No one could swear as to the product's effectiveness, but it did appear to be better than nothing. Late in organizing a motor corps, Toledo would now have one. Mrs. Thomas P. Goodbody announced that she was opening an office in the Spitzer Building, and she hoped drivers would quickly volunteer.

Lorain asked Toledo for atomizers this Saturday, having exhausted its own supply of these sprayers. Lorain's closer neighbor, Cleveland, with an October death rate twenty times normal, could not spare any items in the pharmaceutical line. Also this day, the men, women and children of Toledo were thanked by the needy French, Belgians and Serbians who were wearing shoes they had donated. And, according to the Toledo *News-Bee,* there was something else to be thankful for, as the newspaper headlined: PAIN TAKEN OUT OF CAM-PAIGN. Politicians, as election time neared, would hold no meetings, make no speeches. Health authorities had forbidden this indulgence. That was all there was to it.

Columbus, with twenty-one influenza deaths and 125 new cases, was wrapping Christmas presents for the troops. At 78 East Gay Street, the Red Cross opened a receiving station where it would package and mail parcels overseas. It was suggested that the present first be wrapped, for combined security and utility, in a khaki-colored handkerchief. The parcel, with a maximum allowable weight of three pounds, should contain no matches or "intoxicating liquors."

Construction activity was pushed in Columbus in an effort to beat the ice and snows of approaching winter. The Pennsylvania and the Norfolk and Western freightyards were being expanded, while other steam shovels and laborers with picks were working on the West Side on a flood control project. Residents of the large Ohio city were made aware of the good work of a hundred newly paroled penitentiary inmates, who were reported to be engaged in defense work and essential construction projects. There was, however, scattered criticism of the imposition of influenza measures. "Why," wrote a "housewife" to the *Dispatch*, "do they allow those society women to have their card parties and assemblages in the rooms of the large dry goods stores? Don't you suppose they carry germs as well as the men who congregate in saloons?"

Ohio, all told, had more than 150,000 cases of the flu, which was close to double the number of the previous week. It was a trend epidemiologists found certainly disquieting.

Rochester, like other lake cities, opened its window shades on a bleak, dank morning. Its citizenry was worried; the twenty deaths and four hundred new cases of influenza represented an alarming new high. However, there remained optimism that the epidemic would slack off in time for two principal events on November 4: the arrival of magician Howard Thurston at the Lyceum, and a big sauerkraut dinner of the Germania Chapter 72 at the Masonic Temple. Readers of the *Times-Union* were about to start a series, "Making the Most out of Marriage." And in its advertising columns they learned that "Fruit-a-Tives" probably would help them to resist Spanish influenza.

Further east, it was just as wet and dismal a day in Albany, where 231 had died of influenza in the past week. The employees of the nearby Watervliet Arsenal were especially hurt. Governor Charles S. Whitman was back in the state capital after a campaign tour which the epidemic had only partially interrupted. He had defied the germs to maintain a vigorous offensive against Tammany Hall. The governor-candidate, however, could not speak of unusual prosperity, in spite of war industry in the Empire State. Bradstreet's this very day had itself published glum tidings: the market was slumping. The reason appeared self-evident to financial analysts: ". . . disturbing effect of peace talks, influenza and the warm weather."

And in New York City the day was mild, though the temper of its health commissioner, Dr. Copeland, was not. While seemingly 851 deaths just three days previously should have represented the high-water mark of the epidemic, this was not so. The fatalities continued to hover just under eight hundred while the new cases soared, maintaining an average of more than 5500 a day. In the state 45,000 had perished, the highest average in the nation.

The epidemic was not slackening. Dr. Copeland, weary to the point of distraction, looked around for someone to blame — and his target became fellow doctors. "Continued carelessness of physicians" in late filing of sickness and mortality reports, charged the health commissioner, was resulting in unreliable daily totals. The actual rates may have been lower — or much higher — than represented. He asserted he did not know, while calling attention again to the $500 fines for late reports. It was, through frustration, fear and emotional depletion, a time for recriminations of many sorts, and from many quarters.

"There is a growing conviction," declared the *Scientific American,* "that the sudden invasion of the United States by that European epidemic known as Spanish influenza and the speed with which it has spread throughout the country are due to the laxity with which the port authorities along the Atlantic seaboard have carried out their duties."

And many persons were loud in their demands for better convoy protection by the Navy. This was inspired by the announcement that ships carrying citric acid from Italy and camphor from Japan had been torpedoed in the past few days. There were those, including the medical, who would swear that the two commodities were the only specifics for flu.

Seemingly, with sixty or more dead each day in Newark,

Mayor Gillen had lost his gamble. But it was too late now to admit that possibly he was wrong. He continued "opening up" the city, announcing that schools would ring their bells again on Wednesday.

There were many other signs of civic awakening: The Mt. Pleasant Baptist Church would celebrate the burning of its $30,000 mortgage; while the Women's Missionary Society of the Elizabeth Avenue Baptist Church would meet on Tuesday to discuss "Our Mountaineers." The British American Patriotic Society had rescheduled its autumn dance for November 1, at the New Auditorium. And, so many drivers were back on the streets that traffic accidents were mounting.

Thomas J. Conning was, however, one Newark resident who had reason to wish the saloons had not been reopened. He was hit over the head in one on Market Street and robbed.

By nightfall, Saturday, a week of incalculable devastation had drawn to a close — a week in which more than 21,000 Americans perished from influenza or a combination of influenza and pneumonia. In New York State alone, half a million persons were ill or convalescing.

The Army registered a toll close to that among the civilian population, and already approaching half the number of battle dead. One third of a million soldiers had been ill. The Surgeon General's office, however, believed the killer was nearly tracked down, as it recognized the work of an obscure Rockefeller Institute researcher, reporting:

Dr. Martha Wollstein is very sure that the influenza bacillus is the cause of the present epidemic which she says is due to the respiratory types of the organism as distinguished from the meningeal types occasionally observed in previous years. Dr. Wollstein has not been able to demonstrate any immune bodies to the influenza bacillus in cases of influenza.

But it did not really matter any more whether Martha Wollstein by happenstance, might have cornered the microscopic source of destruction or not. It did not matter whether saloons were open or closed, or if people spat on the sidewalks, forgot to wear face masks, or were shaved in barbershops.

By tomorrow, the residents of Omaha, Minneapolis, Milwaukee, Toledo, Columbus, Rochester, Albany, New York City, Newark and other centers of habitation could schedule bridge parties and church benefits and shop in crowded department stores. They could ride trolleys without the possibility of a policeman ordering them onto the next car. They could soon resume the full trivialities of their lives, for the great epidemic this day was rolling off into the distance like rumbles of a summer thunderstorm.

Wreckage was strewn along its path. But the terrible plague was going. Yet none, certainly not the men or the women of medical science, could say just why it had ceased, any more than they could tell how it had arrived in the first place. They could speculate and question but every answer was merely another frustrating question mark.

19

THE FLU HAD SWEPT past Clearfield on Sunday, October 27, when a record two hundred cases developed in the borough. Then the angel of death had abandoned this Pennsylvania community: one hundred cases on Monday, forty-five on Tuesday . . .

On Tuesday evening, the wall telephone in the office of Dr. Richard Williams in Houtzdale began to ring. Eating supper at the time, he wearily pushed back his chair and stood up. For two weeks, the phone had rung, it seemed, incessantly. The doctor was very tired, for he was county coroner as well as practicing physician.

"Dick," was the voice on the other end, "this is Sam. You better hurry. You understand, don't you?"

Dr. Williams did understand. His friend Dr. Samuel Waterworth was calling from the emergency hospital in Clearfield. Until yesterday, Williams had thought that his sister, Elizabeth Clees, was recovering. Last night she had taken a turn for the worse.

Without attempting to finish his supper, Dr. Williams picked up his black bag — he would certainly have calls to make on his way back — and started his Model T. The evening was dark and cold as he steered over the rutty roads westward, and he wished some kind of stove could be devised for automobiles. However, he made good time, and in slightly more than an hour the yellow, flickering beams of his headlights were picking out the familiar structures of Clearfield. At 9 P.M. he was inside the emergency hospital and at his sister's bedside.

"She's coming along all right now," Dr. Waterworth said, unexpectedly.

Williams looked at his colleague with incredulity.

"Sam, do you really mean this?"

Elizabeth was cyanotic. Her breathing was weak and fitful, her pulse racing and difficult to read.

"Of course I do, Dick," the surgeon persisted.

It was too bad, Williams thought to himself, that doctors had the misguided solicitude which impelled them to try to fool even those of their profession.

Now Jessie Mitchell, a big capable nurse who was acting superintendent of the hospital, arrived by the bed and suggested that Dr. Williams accompany her downstairs for a cup of coffee. Still shivering from the bleak ride, the county coroner thought it an excellent idea.

"Things are improving, Doctor," she told him. "We discharged fifteen patients yesterday."

Dr. Williams found it hard to swallow his coffee. He wasn't sick, but his throat was dry and kept closing up. He felt empty in his stomach, and a strange loneliness was gripping at his entire being.

"You'll excuse me," he finally said. He put down his cup and started up the stairs once more. The smell of carbolic, the sound of people coughing and groaning, the awareness — even to a man who was doctor and coroner — of so much senseless death and misery all at once took possession of him and eroded his scant remaining nervous stamina. All was waste, waste, waste . . .

Miss Mitchell noticed the change which had come over the little physician, and she asked: "Are you all right, Dr. Williams?"

His brow was sweaty when he wiped his hand across it. He steadied himself on the banister of the stairway. But — "Yes," he whispered.

Dr. Williams *knew* when he was several feet from her bedside. Death, in all its many forms, was no stranger to him. Instinctively, he drew his big silver pocket watch out by its massive chain. It was 9:30 o'clock.

"Nurse," he said, still reflectively, "do you have a pencil . . .?"

The word spread quickly through Clearfield. In her home, Ella Fulton, Borough Solicitor John Urey's sweetheart, took out her diary and slowly, haltingly wrote: "Oh, it is so awful to think we will never see her again. I cannot realize it!" She began to cry.

Everybody had loved Nurse Clees. Her death was a very personal thing. She had long been a symbol in the county of selflessness and personal dedication. Stewart, the managing editor of the *Progress*, sat up until 3 A.M. Wednesday writing the story:

> "Peace hath her victories," also her sacrifices. The truth of the above observation was brought home to the people of Clearfield last night when the sad tidings of the death of Mrs. R. K. Clees at the emergency hospital was circulated about the town.
>
> When the Spanish influenza epidemic began here and the health authorities decided to open an emergency hospital for the treatment of the victims of the disease, Mrs. Clees, who before her marriage one year ago was a highly competent trained nurse, was asked to take charge of the same. She

promptly consented, and when the Children's Home was secure immediately took charge as matron or superintendent and in an incredibly short time had that commodious structure converted into a most up-to-date and highly comfortable home for the sick.

No sooner had the hospital been opened than the influx of epidemic victims began. Mrs. Clees worked like a Trojan night and day in those first hours before adequate help could be provided and stopped at no inconvenience or extra effort to make all the sick in her charge as comfortable as possible.

As has been the case in so many instances, the ministering angel herself was stricken and despite heroic efforts to keep going was forced to succumb and take to her bed. The disease ran its usual course and in a few days Mrs. Clees appeared to be improving nicely. Suddenly a change occurred, pneumonia developed and for the past three days and nights this martyr in the cause of suffering humanity carried on a heroic but unequal and inadequate fight for life.

Steadily, the disease progressed, sapping the weakened vitality, despite all that medical skill and tender, careful nursing could devise, until the end came last evening, the supreme sacrifice was exacted and as heroic a soul as ever left the body of soldier or martyr on any battlefield, winged its silent flight to the God who gave it.

No death in Clearfield ever caused more genuine sorrow or regret from the community in general, everybody seeming to feel deeply and keenly that the supreme sacrifice of this good woman was made in the service of each and every citizen of the town and in order that death and sorrow might be kept from each and everyone's fireside.

In Clearfield, tragedy was passing, though the sorrow of which Editor Stewart spoke would linger for a long, long time, in many homes. The *Progress* reported in the same issue: "Yesterday was the quietest day that the undertakers have had since the influenza epidemic started in to reap its harvest." Life was returning to normal faster than anyone only a few short days ago would have believed possible. In Leitzinger

Brothers Department Store new goods were placed on the counters. In Brown's Bootshop, Leonardson's Millinery, in Dooley's Drug Store and the Clearfield Hardware fresh displays cheered up the windows.

Managers of the Globe and the two other theaters, optimistic that they would soon be reopened, took heart and started scrubbing the floors and polishing the seats. The Dimeling Hotel added several new palms to its lobby and, across the street, in the tower of the County Court House, the clock finally was made to tell the right time. It had been an hour fast ever since daylight saving went out the past Saturday. Time, seemingly, had been suspended during the epidemic, and no one cared the hour of the day, or even the day of the week.

The executive committee of the local chapter of the Red Cross met long enough to resolve that "in the death of Mrs. Clees this chapter has lost a valued member and this community an estimable and heroic woman who hesitated not to make the supreme sacrifice that others might be benefited."

On Thursday, the last day of October, John Urey lifted the ban on gatherings to allow all who wished to attend Elizabeth Clees's funeral. The rites were conducted on the front porch of her home on Ogden Street by the Reverend Mr. Reeve.

Though a cold rain pat-patted off a rippling black panoply of umbrellas, many were in attendance: John Urey, Ella Fulton, Mayor Chase, Dr. Stewart, for whom Elizabeth had worked as county TB nurse, her brother Richard, John Rigley and Asbury Lee, who had built the Children's Home, Kim Clees, newly widowed and looking uncomfortable in a blue suit he had rented . . . the people of Clearfield County, the young and the not-so-young, were there.

Intermittently disinfecting his hands with alcohol as he had done through the epidemic, Reeve, with a solemn, drawn face, read the doleful words: "The Lord giveth, and the Lord taketh away. . . ."

Up on the ridge, along the south side of town, diggers were at work again in Clearfield Cemetery. Now, in the drizzle, though already drenched with sweat, they toiled with weary haste over this newest grave. Alternately they shoveled and picked at the rocky soil, their picks thudding through a lonely, consummately dreary pattern against the heavy gray skies, up and down, and up and down. . . .

20

THE "LONESOME OCTOBER" had ended. A cool, bright November arrived to assuage a nation shaken and still trembling. Camphor bottles and jars of pungent salves, aspirin, quinine, rubbing alcohol and all the "influenza specials" went back into America's medicine cabinets. Windows were thrown open, rugs hung out on the line and floors scrubbed. Tens of thousands of face masks became dustcloths. The ragtime beats were plucked out of the record cabinets as the gramophones were cranked up.

Projectors whirred again in the motion picture houses of Chicago, Philadelphia and Washington. Piano accompanists returned with their tinny monotone. Moths emerged from the drapery to flicker through the long, thick beams of light, while the buttery, all-pervading odor of popcorn soon replaced that of carbolic.

In Chicago, Dorothy Gish at last resumed her *Battling Jane;* Mary Pickford struck a martial note in *Johanna Enlists;* and Fred Stone was as funny as ever in *The Goat.* Flo-Flo, who had helped in Washington's emergency hospital, was now in Chicago, kicking and shaking again with her "Perfect 36" chorus in a much more accustomed profession.

Director Wilmer Krusen of Philadelphia's department of health and charities declared that the epidemic "has ceased to exist officially." He conceded it was about time, since the nearly 13,000 deaths in his city placed Philadelphia second in fatalities only to New York. In fact, the figure accounted for more than a third of all Pennsylvania's dead.

Police, in some ways, wished the old restrictions were back. In the first night of the opening of saloons in the City of Brotherly Love, fifty-three fractious persons were arrested for drunkenness and disorderly conduct, setting a record. And, farther down the coast, on the Potomac, a nostalgic sound pleasantly intruded once more: the throaty blast of the S.S. *Charles Macalester*'s whistle. She was an ancient side-wheeler which took excursionists between Washington and Mount Vernon and other river points.

All the theaters reopened with elaborate billings. B. F. Keith's vaudeville demonstrated that while it may have been closed these past weeks, its stage hands were not idle. Elaborate settings and wire supports had been rigged to lend verisimilitude to "An American Ace," in shooting down three Germans. Lew Dockstader completed this bill, one which a variety devotee such as President Wilson could hardly resist. And, in fact, he did not.

Meetings and religious services were resumed without restriction. Dr. Gordon at the First Congregational Church, for example, announced his next Sunday night talk: "Why Did Napoleon Divorce Josephine?"

Commissioner Brownlow and Dr. Mustard had recovered. The former conceded that some good had been salvaged out of the epidemic, as he urged that the staggered government shifts and ten o'clock opening for business houses be continued. It had resulted in appreciably less traffic congestion.

The surgeons general of the Army, Navy and Public Health

Service and the medical director of the Red Cross viewed the burning out of the epidemic with understandably mixed emotions, though the predominant one was frustration. They conceded that they had been able to do nothing positive to stop or even stem the raging disease; indeed, the microbes came and went with such speed that the local organization barely had time to erect elemental defenses. While medical men predicted it might be weeks before the final case of influenza was recorded, it was nonetheless not too soon to commence recapitulating, and thus provide researchers of tomorrow with important tools.

The Navy, it was obvious, had been hurt worst of all. More than 120,000 officers and men, or nearly one fourth of its entire personnel, had been stricken. Five thousand were dead. The fate of the U.S.S. *Pittsburgh*, in Rio harbor, had been shared, in varying measure, by sister vessels. The disease's malice had not been vented singly upon her. The Army lost 25,000 to the tiny, deadly influenza germ. This fighting service, however, was more than ten times the size of its sister sea arm.

At Camp Meade, a huge open-air service was held both as memorial to the flu dead and as a thanksgiving for its deliverance from the pestilence. The impressive services, which left even the exuberant young draftees surprisingly affected, closed with a mass singing of "Onward, Christian Soldiers."

In the first few days of November, remaining areas of infestation returned to health: Pittsburgh, Cleveland, Cincinnati, St. Louis — and San Francisco.

As restless sailors rushed ashore from their long confinement at the Naval Training Station on Goat Island, their medical officers could congratulate themselves that not one case of flu had, in fact, broken through the heavily guarded barriers. The bars of San Francisco, the theaters and even the relatively contaminated atmosphere of their homes, however, now speedily infected a number of those released. The Navy surgeons shrugged. They could not keep the men confined forever. Indeed, they were wearied of the quarantine themselves.

Throughout the nation there was song and prayer. It was as though the lights had been turned on again in a room which had been long dark. The ministers led prayers with renewed and unusual emotion and asked their congregations to promise God they would be better people. Billy Sunday, still in Providence, Rhode Island, gave thanks.

The relief expressed in America was analogous to that of which Defoe had written following the lifting of his plague:

> It is impossible to express the change that appeared in the very countenances of the people . . . it might have been perceived in their countenances that a secret surprise and smile of joy sat on everybody's face. They shook one another by the hands in the streets, who would hardly go on the same side of the way with one another before. Where the streets were not too broad, they would open their windows and call from one house to another, and ask how they did, and if they had heard the good news that the plague was abated . . . they would cry out, "God be praised!" and would weep aloud for joy, telling them they had heard nothing of it; and such was the joy of the people that it was, as it were, life to them from the grave. . . . It pleased God, as it were, by His immediate hand to disarm the enemy; the poison was taken out of the sting. It was wonderful; even the physicians themselves were surprised.

In the first week of November, 1918, though the fiery curse had all but left the United States, the scenes in London appeared much as Defoe had long ago written of that same city. Nearly 14,000 persons perished from influenza this week in England. It was more than twice the birth rate — a statistic of marked implications.

"There is," wrote *The Times*, "no sensible diminution yet

in the number of fresh cases of influenza." In London, accounting for one third of all the epidemic fatalities in the British Isles, the sick and dead were found upon the streets, as in the great plagues of yesterday. Policemen and firemen were ill and even the primary necessity for keeping clean was difficult of realization: the Launderers Association announced it was refusing all wash, since its help were ill. More and more Britons demanded a "Health Ministry" as one protection. "Only a few miserable thousands were spent by the nation on research work and we are paying the penalty," stormed Sir Kingsley Wood. Recriminations volleyed and thundered. And the germs continued to kill people.

Residents of Dublin died at the rate of 250 a day. In Barcelona, with 100,000 ill, the morbidity was not much less than in Ireland. Paris was ailing in the same proportions as London. Train service between Berlin and Sweden had been suspended, but not because of the war. There were no crews well enough to operate them. Prince Max of Baden, the new German chancellor, who had been actively seeking an armistice, went to bed with a high fever. Now more than ever did the rulers of this unhappy Middle European nation regret the war for which they must share at least a portion of the creative credit. The land of the Nile was not overlooked by the plague. Ezra bin Abbas, heir apparent of the khedive of Egypt, died on the first day of November.

Then, on November 10, after two thousand persons perished in Britain's "great cities" in the flickering of twenty-four hours, or even less, a miracle seemingly happened. The suffering was ceasing. With the signing of the Armistice, the epidemic in England — and in Europe — commenced a downward plunge, even as it had in the United States in late October. It was, at least, coincidence.

On a foggy, cold Monday morning November 11, an announcement was chalked on a window along the Boulevard des Capucines in Paris:

L'ARMISTICE EST SIGNÉ
LA GUERRE EST GAGNÉE
VIVE LA FRANCE! VIVENT LES ALLIÉS!
LES HOSTILITÉS ONT CESSÉ À 11 HEURES

Crazy with victory, Parisians raced through the streets, shouting, singing, laughing, occasionally even praying, and kissing, as they converged on the Place de la Concorde. The correspondent of *The Times* wrote: "The din under the windows of *The Times* is so great that it is almost impossible to dictate this telegram."

In London, the King and Queen appeared on the balcony of Buckingham Palace to acknowledge the cheers of nearly a million of their subjects who had been waiting patiently in the rain for several hours. The Irish Guards band blared forth "Rule, Britannia!"

Weary, sorrowing from the long attrition by war and disease, Britons nonetheless rallied as the day wore on. By afternoon, huge bonfires — fueled by advertising boards snatched from passing omnibuses — were crackling in Trafalgar Square. For once, the pigeons were forced to quit their habitual roost upon the lions or even the Nelson column itself.

"Nightfall," reported *The Times*, "brought no end to the public jubilation. The unceasing drizzle was powerless to depress the high spirits of the people. In some of those places where merrymakers are mostly to be found, the street lamps had been unmasked. The porticoes of several of the theaters were ablaze with lights. Overhead, the searchlights played."

The mood of London, one of immense relief, seemed expressed in a hastily wrought straw effigy of the Kaiser which was trundled down Oxford Street towards Piccadilly Circus, above the scrawled placard: GONE TO A BETTER 'OLE.

Across the Atlantic, the time difference was responsible for a celebration which commenced before dawn. In many cities, factory whistles, church and fire bells and even the shooting of pistols and small-caliber rifles awakened the citizenry from sleep. By midmorning, every populous center of the United States was wildly acclaiming the end of the nation's venture into the Great War. There was a "monstrous discord" in Chicago's Loop as men, women and children donned costumes to parade in New Orleans fashion. Even the 16,000 police called to duty couldn't entirely preserve order.

There were similar demonstrations in New York, where any soldier or sailor who ventured into Times Square was besieged by kissing-happy women as though they assumed that any man in uniform had personally brought about the downfall of the Kaiser.

"From every street and highway," wrote the *Philadelphia Inquirer*, "from every quarter and purlieu, from the stately mansions of the rich, from the modest homes and lodgings of the workers, from the alleys and the courts of the lowly and the poor, its multitude poured forth."

In Washington, President Wilson adjusted his pince-nez and informed a joint session of Congress that the war had ended, then read the Armistice terms. A wooden platform was being knocked together in front of the White House from which the Chief Executive would review the capital's own victory parade. The noise and excitement continued in America into the night.

The churches of Pittsburgh struck an unusual mood in vespers as their carillons played "Johnny Get Your Gun" and "Over There." At least the notes dinned out the clatter of tens of thousands of tin cans over cobblestone which overzealous young boys had tied to the tails of the city's dogs and cats. Lillian Russell, a Pittsburgh resident, appeared in a "Victory Act" at the Davis Theater. Middle age, the epidemic and a Victorian quality about her dramatic style had recently taken toll of her potential bookings.

To the east, Clearfield, where grief had come into so many homes, found spirit to celebrate. Fire trucks ranged through the borough, their bells clanging. Empty oil drums were placed on wagons and crowbars employed as impromptu but effective drumsticks. No one paid heed to a steady drizzle. The bell of the Reverend Mr. Reeve's church was rung so constantly and so exuberantly that the cord broke. While his three-year-old daughter Rebecca held the ladder, the minister clambered up into the belfry and affixed a new rope. The cheery clangor resumed, with unfamiliar abandon.

> The racket and din kept up [reported the *Progress*]. The parade at 7:30 was a magnificent spectacle and was participated in by several hundred automobiles, several thousand wildly enthusiastic citizens. Mayor Chase with Marshal John M. Bain, Jack Eadie and C. E. Hoover were in charge and they handled the big mob in a highly capable manner.
>
> The principal streets were traversed and when the march was finished at the court house corner the streets four ways from the diamond were a solid mass of humanity.
>
> All were good natured, nor did they have much if any artificial encouragement to get gay and make merry.

There were, of course, many who did not participate in the day's or the night's revelry. There were those still abed, and those still submerged in the wonderment and despair of recent loss.

Among the latter was Kim Clees. This round, bespectacled man sat in his parlor on Ogden Street surrounded, as always, by clocks and the mechanisms of clocks. With a masklike expression, typical of the little man whom all in Clearfield knew but few understood, he worked this night of the Armistice on the objects of his trade, or at least one of his trades.

Upon the walls of the dimly lit room, hung against the fading, streaking rose print paper, carelessly pegged above, below, and flanking the motto bequeathed by an earlier tenant, "God Bless Our Home," upon the tables, chairs, and even strewn about the floor and atop the worn rag rug were clocks, and parts of clocks, and more clocks — cuckoo clocks, French clocks, simple, flat-faced wind-up clocks, kitchen clocks, alarm clocks and even water clocks.

Those which still ran tick-tocked, tick-tocked away in mute, continuing testimony to the enigma of time and the heartbreak often left in its passage.

Yet, even as Kim Clees fussed with his microscopic implements and parts, another manifestation of time's harvest became lustily apparent. In the Clearfield Hospital, these last minutes of November 11, 1918, there intruded a sound of never-ending wonder, the cry of newborn babies, two in number. Life, tenacious and indestructible as it was mysterious, would continue. The fury of neither man nor nature would stanch its forward surge.

Epilogue

LATE INTO 1919, delayed reports of the epidemic's ravages in isolated lands reached the world's capitals. A school-teacher named Evans of Nome, Alaska, for example, advised Washington:

> Ten villages this district affected. Three wiped out entirely, others average 85 per cent deaths . . . total number of deaths reported 750, probably 25 per cent this number froze to death before help arrived. Over 300 children to be cared for, majority of whom are orphans. Am feeding and caring for surviving population of five large villages.

For months, the residents of Fairbanks were subject to periodic checkups and required to wear armbands marked "OK, FAIRBANKS HEALTH DEPARTMENT." Those found without bands were quarantined in jail.

Belated flareups or deaths attributed to the past year's epidemic were also evident in Puerto Rico and in revolution-torn Hamburg, Germany, where jute sacks now took the place of coffins and furniture vans doubled for hearses. The natives of New Guinea were forced to submit to vaccination. The Kanaka tribe, steeped in witchcraft, became docile under the hypodermic needle only after members were convinced that the injection was a good spirit which would fight off their traditional devil or evil spirit *"tamarang."*

Otherwise, "the most lethal pandemic in history" was being relegated to the vale of research and afterthought. It persisted as the despair of the world's medical profession, a nagging, not-to-be-dismissed challenge and a wellspring of self-recrimination. The devastation, concluded Dr. Kenneth F. Maxcy, of the United States Public Health Service, had been "an appalling demonstration of man's helplessness and ignorance." The economic loss was incalculable, for none could produce a reasonable yardstick of the value to the community or the nation of each and every victim of the flu. Nor were statistics available as to just how many private enterprises had failed because of the deaths of their owners, how much production in the broader fields had been sacrificed because of lost man hours or, certainly, loss in skills through the altered careers of tens of thousands of children hurt financially because of the deaths of their parents.

The Metropolitan Life Insurance Company was one signal exception. It was in a position to know immediately what the pandemic had wrought within its own orderly business. The probability tables worked out by the best mathematical brains in the actuarial science had been made a mockery for, in a few months, Metropolitan had paid out more than $18 million in initial demands from the beneficiaries of 85,000 policies. In the history of the world's insurers, there had been nothing to equal such a Niagara of claims.

However, freed of the immediate distractions of the epidemic, epidemiologists were now able, leisurely and with detachment, to retrace the path of the tornado of infection.

There was, finally, agreement that influenza was caused by its own peculiar germ, and none other — one capable of continuing mutations, as elusive as an eel, as difficult to recognize as a passerby at midnight. Martha Wollstein herself had arrived at these conclusions in the sputtering hours of New York's epidemic. Influenza, it had become generally conceded, was a virus — a microscopic, filterable microbe.

As to the origins of the pandemic, or its initial invasion routes, there was no accord. The United States, France and China loomed as the most likely spawning grounds. Dr. Warren T. Vaughan of the Harvard Medical School and son of the recent Acting Surgeon General, Dr. Victor Vaughan, dated the earliest 1918 epidemic in the United States as having appeared in Camp Funston, at Fort Riley, Kansas, on March 5, and added, "We are inclined to conclude that it was carried to France with the great body of men traveling to that country from the United States." The particular virus, he continued, possessed "sufficient virulence to produce the pandemic." Others advanced his thinking a step further, revolving around the war-induced melting pot of people and races in France. "It might be argued," went the theory, "that a vicious new hybrid virus had been born in that very mixed culture."

Nor were those familiar with chemistry apt to doubt the earlier belief that the high explosives of war, its gases — direct and secondary — and other byproducts of its violence, such as dust from shattered buildings, could alter the virus. It was, like all matter — animate or inanimate — merely a chemical structure in itself.

Not until 1933, nonetheless, was the killer partially cornered. Appropriately, London, the scene of the virus's especial ravages, became the area of seeming medical victory — the location, the National Institute for Medical Research at suburban Hampstead.

"Ferret Number One looks somewhat seedy" was the laconic announcement on February 4, 1933, by Professor Wilson Smith, of the institute. Together with Professor W. W. C. Topley,

195

Patrick P. ("P.P.") Laidlaw and Dr. Christopher H. Andrewes, Smith had found an unwitting hero in this possibly nastiest of all rodents: the ferret. It had been discovered that the influenza then occurring could be transmitted artificially to ferrets. It was simultaneously learned, information hitherto purely speculative, that the nasal passages were the microbe's sole route of entry.

Within four weeks, the exultant medical team had so many sick ferrets that one of its members, Professor Smith himself, came down with the flu. A feverish ferret had sneezed in the researcher's face. The experiments met with such eminent success that ferrets began to die as if another plague year had in fact arrived. "Fortunately," observed Dr. Andrewes, "we still had plenty of ferrets."

Within two years, the ability to induce influenza in ferrets had been extended to mice, and serums were being developed. The triumph at Hampstead had also given impetus to influenza research throughout the world. In 1935, a "moderate outbreak" of influenza presented its own opportunities for directed laboratory research, now that the villain had been, to some extent, unmasked. Five years later, it was established that influenza was divided into two major strains, "A" and "B," with suprisingly little relationship between them.

At about this time, the electron microscope was introduced commercially. The influenza virus was at last made to pose for its "mugging" portrait, like any apprehended criminal. It turned out to be disarmingly mild in appearance — a fluffy, cotton-like ball. They were so tiny, however, that twenty or thirty million of them could fit on the head of a pin, and not crowd.

How they multiplied so rapidly none could say. It was established, however, that their first targets in the human were the epithelial cells, in turn almost as invisible as the virus itself. Once these cells were broken down, all bodily functions ground to a halt, much like an expensive watch which has been attacked by rust. The more the mechanism resists, the more rapid and inevitable becomes final collapse.

The question persisted, however, now that epidemiologists knew what the virus looked like: what is the character of Spanish influenza?

World War II came along, and presented its own acute challenges in the realm of medical problems. Spectacular advances marked not only battlefield surgery but the offensive against disease in remote corners of the world.

Not until long after the war, in 1951, did a medical team finally attempt the obvious in the still earnest quest for the seemingly lost Spanish influenza virus. Led by Dr. Albert P. McKee of the State University of Iowa, a group of researchers journeyed to Alaska. There they exhumed the bodies, preserved within the permafrost line of the icy earth, of several Eskimo victims of the 1918 epidemic. Lung sections were packed in ice and sent back to Iowa City in an effort to infect laboratory animals.

The potential of this endeavor was great. *If* the virus still existed in its own latent and mysterious state of quasi-animation, it could possibly be classified, and mankind might be spared another visitation. The virus, however, could not be recovered. Like a murderer in the night, it had not tarried over its victims. Where, indeed, had it gone?

Now, however, a World Influenza Center had been established at Mill Hill near London by the World Health Organization. Its director was Dr. Andrewes, the sole surviving member of the group which had isolated influenza in 1933. He himself indirectly answered the questions posed as to the disappearance of the Spanish influenza strain. Commenting on the known "A" virus, Dr. Andrewes noted:

Most people believe it goes, metaphorically speaking, "underground." It is rarely recovered from "flu-like" illnesses between epidemics. There is a strong suggestion, however, that it can persist in an area without causing outbreaks . . . I can believe that virus goes underground and perhaps does so all over the world, causing odd subclinical infections and not much more, but able to become active and epidemic when the time is ripe.

On other scores, he added:

We cannot, unfortunately, say that influenza is yet a certainly preventable disease and it is still possible that a pandemic might return and kill its millions, as happened in 1918-19. . . . The variation of the virus is not yet fully understood, nor are its movements which are so important from the epidemiologists point of view.

Sir Frank MacFarlane Burnet, a leading Australian microbiologist, seconded Dr. Andrewes's observations himself in 1952:

Of all the virus diseases, influenza is probably that in which mutational changes in the virus are of greatest human importance. We can only guess what type of virus was responsible in 1918-19 and what changes took place during the course of the pandemic. But even in the period since the human virus was first isolated in 1933 there have been striking changes in the immunological character of both influenza "A" and "B" viruses. Some of us believe that the influenza virus' chief means of survival is its capacity for constant mutation to new serological patterns, and those of us who have had anything to do with the production of influenza vaccines know very well how that capacity can nullify the most painstaking work. . . .

No one yet can say whether or when we shall see another pandemic outbreak of influenza. Until we know the answer to that question we should not be too complacent about our powers to deal with acute infectious disease.

Institutes such as the World Influenza Center and the National Institute of Health in Washington were as well prepared for epidemic as any organization can be when the "Asian flu" arrived in 1957. Some concluded that the world-wide bacteriological equivalent of an air-raid warning network had much to do with the control of this recent microbe visitation. Effective vaccines were not long in appearing.

However, this was Asian flu, not Spanish influenza. Indeed, the humility of researchers had to be maintained, for who could say whether the course or intensity of this outbreak would have been any different with only such basic treatments as were accorded the victims of 1918? Would the alcohol rubs, the aspirin, quinine, hot soups and pneumonia jackets have served almost as effectively?

Influenza, while in some forms identified, photographed and challenged by vaccines, is nonetheless as tricky as the common cold and apparently as impossible to stamp out. As late as the spring of 1960, this bulletin was published by the epidemiology division of the Canadian Department of National Health and Welfare:

> An outbreak of influenza-like disease has been reported at Slave Lake in the Northwest Territories. About 20 per cent of the population were affected beginning about March 24 and ending April 10. Whole families were ill at the same time and all ages were affected except infants under 6 months of age. At Coppermine, also in the Northwest Territories, which has a population of 228 Eskimos and 47 white persons, 81 per cent of the former and 47 per cent of the latter were affected in an epidemic. Forty-five persons had to be admitted to a hospital and of these, 35 had pulmonary complications. A second outbreak has occurred at Pelly Bay where one infant and three adults died.

It read with familiar overtones, sounding almost as though Spanish influenza was on the prowl again.

Acknowledgments

The author is indebted to the following people: Dr. Christopher H. Andrewes, Director, Wold Influenza Center; Gertrude L. Annan, New York Academy of Medicine; Mrs. Blanche D. Beattie, Granville, Ohio; Gordon L. Beck, Winona Lake Bible Conference; Cecil Bloom, Clearfield, Pennsylvania; Louis Brownlow, Washington, D. C.; Clyde Buckingham, American National Red Cross, Washington; Mrs. Ernest A. Burrill, Brockton, Massachusetts; Dr. Leoni N. Claman, New York Infirmary; W. A. Clees, McKeesport, Pennsylvania; Dr. George W. Corner, Rockefeller Institute; Miss Mabel E. Davis, Brockton, Massachusetts; Miss Dorothy Deming, former editor, *Public Health Nursing;* M. Ellis, The Admiralty, London; Mrs. Henrietta Freeman, San Francisco; M. B. Fretz, editor-publisher, *The Newberry News;* Miss Janet Geister, nurse-author, Chicago; Dr. Connie M. Guion, New York; Mrs. Gladys Haggerty, Hollywood; Lieutenant Colonel Elizabeth Harding, ANC (Ret.); Dr. John F. Hogan, Baltimore; Mrs. June Holes, American Red Cross, Clearfield Chapter; Mrs. Greta Lindblad Holmberg, Brockton, Massachusetts; Mrs. Glenn I. Jones, Washington; Eugene H. Kone, Rockefeller Institute; Colonel Milford T. Kubin, Irwin Hospital, Fort Riley, Kansas; Dr. James

P. Leake, Washington; Mrs. Kathryn Clees McGeehin, Enola, Pennsylvania; Dr. Rustin McIntosh, The Presbyterian Hospital; Dr. Peter K. Olitsky, Greenwich, Connecticut; Lee Rich, Manager, *The Junction City Daily Union,* Junction City, Kansas; Rev. Edward Reeve, Clearfield; Mrs. Franklin D. Roosevelt; Barbara Schutt, R.N., Editor, *American Journal of Nursing;* Dr. Charles Hendee Smith, Princeton; Gilbert S. Terrell, American National Red Cross; John Urey and Mrs. Ella Fulton Urey, Clearfield; Mrs. Dorothy K. Whyte, Metropolitan Life Insurance Company; Dr. Huntington Williams, Commissioner of Health, Baltimore; Dr. Richard Williams, Houtzdale; Rear Admiral Ellis M. Zacharias, USN (Ret.)

The author is especially grateful to the National Institutes of Health, United States Department of Health, Education and Welfare, for reviewing this book for technical accuracy. Dr. Leake, who played his own essential and selfless role in 1918 and is in the seemingly anomalous position of active retired public health physician and researcher, gave generously of his time to check the manuscript. Donald Goldthorpe, information officer with the infectious diseases division of the department, is among others in this specialized field of epidemiology who worked patiently to guard the author from the many pitfalls of an unfamiliar realm of the documentary.

The author particularly wishes to express his gratitude to Arthur H. Thornhill, Jr., general manager of Little, Brown, who conceived the original idea for doing a documentary of the 1918 influenza epidemic.

These libraries and reference centers were especially helpful:
The American National Red Cross; Boston Public Library; California Historical Society; Connecticut State Library; Denver Public Library; Grand Rapids Public Library; Harvard College Library; Library of Congress; National Archives; Na-

tional Institutes of Health; National Library of Medicine; New York Public Library; Philadelphia Public Library; Enoch Pratt Free Library (Baltimore); Franklin D. Roosevelt Library, Hyde Park; Washington (District of Columbia) Public Library.

These newspapers and magazines provided valuable background information:

Albany (N.Y.) *Times Union; Atlanta Journal; Baltimore Post; Baltimore Sun; Boston Globe; Boston Herald; Chicago Tribune; Christian Science Monitor; Cincinnati Enquirer; Clearfield Progress; Cleveland Plain Dealer; Columbus Dispatch; Denver Post; Detroit Free Press; Hartford Courant; Kansas City Star;* London *Times; Los Angeles Times; Manchester Guardian; Milwaukee Journal; Newark Evening News; New York Herald; New York Times; Omaha World; Philadelphia Bulletin; Philadelphia Inquirer; Pittsburgh Post; Pittsburgh Press; Providence Journal; Richmond Times-Dispatch; San Francisco Bulletin; San Francisco Chronicle; St. Louis Post Dispatch; Toledo Blade; Washington Post; Evening Star* (Washington).

American Journal of Nursing; American Medical Association Journal, and the many AMA affiliate state and city medical publications; *British Medical Journal; Canadian Medical Association Journal; Collier's; Current History; Illustrated London News; Independent Industrial Arts; Journal American Institute of Homeopathy; Journal of Experimental Medicine; Literary Digest; Living Age; Nursing Outlook; Ohio Public Health Journal; Outlook; Public Health Nurse; Red Cross Magazine;* World Influenza Center publications; *World's Work.*

Bibliography

Aldrich, Mildred. *When Johnny Comes Marching Home.* Small Maynard, Boston, 1919.

Aloe, Col. Alfred. *Twelfth US Infantry.* Members of the 12th US Infantry, 1919.

Barkley, John Lewis. *No Hard Feelings.* Cosmopolitan Book Corp., New York, 1930.

Baron, A. L. *Man Against Germs.* Dutton, New York, 1957.

Benwell, Harry. *History of the Yankee Division.* Cornhill, Boston, 1919.

Burnet, Sir Frank MacFarlane. *The Virus and the Cell.* Government Printing Office, Washington, 1952.

Cook, J. Gordon. *Virus in the Cell.* Dial Press, New York, 1957.

Cooper, Page. *The Bellevue Story.* Crowell, New York, 1948.

Corday, Michel. *The Paris Front.* Dutton, New York, 1934.

Defoe, Daniel. *A Journal of the Plague Year.* Longmans Green, London, 1895.

Dock, Lavinia L. and others. *History of American Red Cross Nursing.* Macmillan, New York, 1922.

Dublin, Dr. Louis I. *Twenty-five Years of Health Progress.* Metropolitan Life Insurance Co., New York, 1937.

Gorgas, Marie D. *William Crawford Gorgas: His Life and Work*. Doubleday Page, Garden City, 1924.

Harbord, James G. *The American Army in France, 1917-1919*. Little, Brown, Boston, 1936.

Hare, Ronald. *Pomp and Pestilence*. Philosophical Library, New York, 1955.

Holden, Frank A. *War Memories*. Athens Book Co., Athens, Georgia, 1922.

Howard, Dr. William Travis, Jr. *Public Health Administration and the Natural History of Disease in Maryland*. Carnegie Institution, 1924.

Jordan, Edwin O. *Epidemic Influenza*. American Medical Association, Chicago, 1927.

Lamb, Albert R. *The Presbyterian Hospital and the Columbia-Presbyterian Medical Center*. Columbia University Press, New York, 1955.

March, Peyton C. *The Nation at War*. Doubleday Doran, Garden City, 1932.

Ministry of Health, Great Britain. *Reports on Public Health and Medical Subjects — No. 4*. His Majesty's Stationery Office, London, 1920.

Order of Battle of the United States Land Forces in the World War, 1917-1919. U. S. Government Printing Office, 1949.

Palmer, Frederick. *Newton D. Baker: America at War*. Dodd Mead, New York, 1931.

Paul, Dr. Hugh. *The Control of Communicable Diseases*. Harvey & Blythe, London, 1952.

Pearl, Dr. Raymond. *Influenza*. U. S. Public Health Service, Government Printing Office, 1919.

Pfeiffer, Dr. Richard. *Vorläufige Mittheilungen über die Erreger de Influenza*. Institute for Infectious Diseases, Berlin, 1892.

Pressley, Harry T. *Saving the World for Democracy*. Artcraft Co., Clarinda, Iowa, 1933.

Ross, Leland. *This Democratic Roosevelt*. Dutton, New York, 1932.

Smith, Geddes. *Plague on Us*. The Commonwealth Fund, New York, 1941.

Starr, John. *Hospital City*. Crown, New York, 1957.

Taylor, Major Emerson Gifford. *New England in France*. Houghton Mifflin, Boston, 1920.

Thompson, Dr. Theophilus. *Annals of Influenza*. The Sydenham Society, London, 1852.

Vaughan, Victor C. *Epidemiology and Public Health*. Mosby, St. Louis, 1922.

Vaughan, Warren T. "Influenza." *American Journal of Hygiene*, Baltimore, 1921.

Vermont in the World War. Free Press, Burlington, 1920.

Wald, Lillian D. *Windows on Henry Street*. Little, Brown, Boston, 1941.

Index

Wald, Lillian, 49, 81, 87-88, 98
Waldbauer, Lewis J., 81
Wales, Claude A., 25
Washington, D.C., emergency measures, 53-55; crippling effects on, 59, 75; precautionary efforts, 75, 76-77; *Evening Star*, 90, 136; hospital facilities, 94; deaths, 136
Washington Trust Co., 166
Waterworth, Dr. Samuel, 178
Watervliet Arsenal, 174
Watkins (N.Y.), 42
Watson, William, 132
Waynesburg (Pa.), 145
Welch, Dr. William, 27
West Side Hospital (Chicago), 44
West Virginia, 46
Westinghouse Electric Co., 146
Westphal, Mary E., 148
White, W. H., Jr., 115
Whitechapel (London), 157
Whitman, Gov. Charles S., 174
Wilhelm, Emperor, 19
Wilkes-Barre (Pa.), 52
Williams, E. L., 127

Williams, Dr. Richard, 135, 178-180
Williams, Rev. Robert G., 69, 70
Williamson, Mrs. Gertrude, 53
Wilmington (Del.), 46
Wilson, President Woodrow, 54, 55-56, 185, 190
Winnetka (Ill.), 44
Winthrop (Mass.), 41
Wisely, Dr. Edward D., 141
Wollstein, Dr. Martha, 47-48, 86-87, 141, 167, 176, 195
Wood, Sir Kingsley, 188
Woodbury (N.J.), 81
Woodson, Mrs. Ann Olds, 123
Woodward, Dr. William C., 26
World Health Organization, 197
World Influenza Center, 197, 199
"Wrestler's fever," 20

Yacona, 159
Yankee Division, 27
York (Pa.), 95
Y.M.C.A., 64, 93

Zacharias, Lt. Ellis M., 128